101 Gourmet
cakes

WENDY PAUL

FRONT TABLE BOOKS
AN IMPRINT OF CEDAR FORT, INC.
SPRINGVILLE, UTAH

ISBN: 978-1-4621-1388-0

Published by Front Table Books, an imprint of Cedar Fort, Inc.

2373 W. 700 S., Springville, UT, 84663

Distributed by Cedar Fort, Inc., www.cedarfort.com

LIBRARY OF CONGRESS CATALOGING-IN-PUBLICATION DATA

Paul, Wendy, author.

101 gourmet cakes simply from scratch / Wendy Paul.

p. cm.

ISBN 978-1-4621-1388-0

I. Cake. I. Title. II. Title: One hundred one gourmet cakes simply from scratch. III. Title: One hundred and one gourmet cakes simply from scratch.

TX771.P38 2014

641.86'53—dc23

2014010278

Cover design by Erica Dixon

Page design by Bekah Claussen

Cover design © 2014 by Lyle Mortimer

Edited by Rachel J. Munk

Printed in China

10 9 8 7 6 5 4 3 2 1

Dedication

Without you, I would have nothing. Thank you for sacrificing your waistlines to make this book the best it could be. I love you all.

P.S. Plus—the more you eat, the thinner I feel.

Contents

Holiday Treats

Let's Eat Cake!

"A PARTY WITHOUT CAKE IS JUST A MEETING." —Julia Child

IN THE PROCESS OF MAKING and researching recipes, I have come across and tasted some pretty amazing cakes. So it seemed a natural progression in this 101 Gourmet Series to make book all about wonderful cakes. Why not? I can't seem to stop baking.

THERE ARE SOME PRETTY TASTY CREATIONS in this book. From classics like Strawberry Lemon Shortcake to Pineapple Upside Down Cake, German Chocolate Cake to Banana Skillet Cake. Then I threw in some fun and exciting new flavors, like Chocolate Mousse Cake, Cannoli Cream Cake, and an amazing Key Lime Cheesecake.

WITH SO MANY OPTIONS for a beautiful and tasty cake, you can make whatever your heart desires. Or whatever your friends and family desire. With these easy, from-scratch recipes, anyone can be successful in the kitchen. After all, most of our memories go hand in hand with good food. And, more important, with yummy cake.

HAPPY BAKING!

Wendy L. Paul

Tips for Success

CAKE-MAKING TOOLS

The basic must-haves in the kitchen are:
- Offset spatula
- Cake decorating bags or plastic bags
- Large bell whisk
- Parchment paper
- 9-inch round cake pans, at least a set of 2
- Springform pan

THE BASICS OF FONDANT

Fondant is a sugar dough that is used to cover and decorate cakes. You most often see fondant on wedding cakes. It creates a smooth, beautiful texture, making a show-stopper of a cake. Homemade fondant tastes much better than store bought, although I've found that store bought fondant works great as well. Because it can be easily stored for multiple uses, fondant is a great ingredient to have on hand. There are two general recipes for fondant that I love that do the trick for any cake decorating. Granted, if I had my choice, I'd choose buttercream over fondant any day, but you do need a great fondant recipe to work with when decorating cakes.

Easy Fondant

½ cup butter, softened

½ cup light corn syrup

1 tsp. vanilla extract

pinch of salt

1½ lb. powdered sugar

IN A MEDIUM BOWL (I use my stand mixer with a paddle attachment), mix together butter, syrup, vanilla, and salt for 1–2 minutes. Gradually add powdered sugar and mix until a soft dough forms, 2–3 minutes. Keep dough wrapped in plastic wrap in an airtight container for up to 2 weeks.

TO ADD COLOR, knead 2–3 drops food coloring (I recommend using plastic food-safe gloves) at a time until desired color is reached.

TO COVER THE CAKES, roll out fondant in a large circle, several inches larger than your cake. I like my fondant thin, but still substantial enough to cover imperfections. Frost your cake with a layer of buttercream frosting, then place the center of the fondant over the center of the cake, gently laying it down to make contact with the cake. The frosting will act like a glue for the fondant. Smooth out with the side of your hand to adhere the fondant to the cake. Trim excess fondant. Decorate as desired.

SHAPES: cookie cutters are essential to shaping fondant easily.

Easy Marshmallow Fondant

¼ cup butter, softened
16 oz. mini marshmallows
¼ cup water
1 tsp. vanilla extract (or other flavoring)
2 lb. powdered sugar

IN A MICROWAVE-SAFE DISH, melt marshmallows. Stir in water and flavoring carefully, since marshmallows will be very hot. Once stirred together completely, add powdered sugar and mix (I like using my stand mixer) until dough comes together but is still sticky. Remove dough and, using the soft butter, coat your hand and knead by hand until pliable. Cover with plastic wrap and place in an airtight container for up to several weeks.

MAKING YOUR CAKE LEVEL

In some cases, your cake may bake with a rounded top. To make it more even, take a bread knife or serrated knife and trim horizontally, taking just the top off the cake to make it completely level. Less is always better at this point. Your cake will then stack evenly when adding multiple layers.

PERFECT BUTTERCREAM FROSTING

Just a few tips for perfect buttercream frosting: Using fresh ingredients is key. Unsalted butter is a must, and the more you whip the white buttercream frosting, the whiter it becomes. Air is such a magical ingredient in buttercream frosting. I always like to whip my frosting on high for just a few more minutes once I get the consistency needed. And always add your flavoring and coloring after the buttercream is perfected.

STORING CAKES

If I know a cake is going to be eaten within two days I usually keep it on the counter, covered and sealed so it won't dry out. A cake plate with a lid does the trick, and it's pretty to look at. If your cake has fresh berries in it, keep it refrigerated. Your cake will last up to one week in the fridge. Cakes will also last up to several months in the freezer.

FREEZING CAKES

You can freeze your cakes for up to several months, but I don't know how cake could ever survive that long—we eat ours so fast! I like to wrap my cooled and unfrosted cakes in plastic wrap, and then seal them in labeled freezer bags. You can then pull out your unfrosted cake and frost it once it comes back to room temperature. This will save time for larger events. You can also freeze cakes after they are frosted; just be sure to seal them after the frosting has set so you don't have messed-up frosting on your cake.

CUTTING AND SERVING CAKES

It's best to invest in a nice cake plate if you are going to be making a lot of cakes. Some of my favorites are those that I've found at consignment stores or those of my grandmothers. I like simple plates, which allow the beautiful cakes to shine and take center stage. It's always nice to have a special serving knife or cake knife. These are usually serrated and have one wide serving side.

CAKE FLOUR OR ALL-PURPOSE FLOUR?

Is there a difference? Yes, there is. Cake flour is high in starch and low in protein. The proteins in all-purpose flour cause a cake to be tough if the batter is overmixed, and cake flour helps to minimize this. Using cake flour can make a big difference in how tender your cakes are. But not everyone has cake flour in their pantry. Almost all of my recipes call for all-purpose flour. If you want to substitute for cake flour in my recipes, just substitute 1 cup minus 2 tablespoons of all-purpose flour for 1 cup of cake flour. One tip to making sure your cakes are not tough: Don't overmix the batter. Don't walk away from your mixer or answer a phone call; just stir the batter until just combined.

ALL OF MY RECIPES USE ALL-PURPOSE FLOUR UNLESS OTHERWISE STATED

Fruity and Fabulous

The Hummingbird

This cake has been around for generations. Here's a slightly healthier version, with all the same flavor and texture you've always loved.

1 ½ cups flour

1 ½ cups whole wheat flour

1 ¼ cup sugar

1 cup shredded coconut

1 tsp. baking soda

1 tsp. baking powder

1 tsp. cinnamon

pinch of salt

3 eggs

1 cup vegetable oil

¾ cup milk

1 tsp. black walnut flavoring (optional)

1 tsp. vanilla bean paste or vanilla extract

2 bananas, mashed

1 (8-oz.) can crushed pineapple with juice

½ cup finely chopped walnuts for garnish

1 recipe Cream Cheese Buttercream Frosting (p. 138)

MIX TOGETHER dry ingredients: flour, sugar, coconut, baking soda, baking powder, cinnamon, and salt. Set aside.

IN ANOTHER BOWL, mix together eggs, oil, milk, walnut flavoring (optional), vanilla, bananas, and pineapple. Add wet ingredients to dry ingredients and stir until smooth and combined.

POUR BATTER into two 9-inch cake pans lined with parchment paper, lightly greased and floured. Bake at 350 degrees for 26–28 minutes until a toothpick comes out clean. Remove from the oven and cool completely. Frost sides and middle of cake. Sprinkle with more finely chopped walnuts for garnish, if desired.

The Hummingbird

Strawberry Lemon Shortcake

I love strawberry shortcake. I wanted to update this classic treat to a large cake, and add one of my favorite flavors of all time—lemon. By adding the lemon curd to the layers of cake before the cream, this cake becomes a most special treat.

2½ cups flour

3 tsp. baking powder

1 tsp. baking soda

1¼ cup sugar

pinch of Kosher salt

1 cup butter, cold

3 eggs, room temperature

1 cup milk room temperature

2 tsp. almond extract

1 tsp. vanilla bean paste (or vanilla extract)

¾ cup butter, softened and cut into cubes

1 recipe Lemon Curd (on following page)

1 recipe Stiff Whipped Cream (p. 124)

2 cups fresh strawberries, sliced (if you need to sweeten the strawberries, add 2 Tbsp. sugar and let sit for 5 minutes)

IN A MEDIUM BOWL, combine flour, baking powder, baking soda, sugar, and salt. Stir to combine.

IN A SEPARATE BOWL, combine eggs and milk, then break each egg, stirring to combine. Add almond extract and vanilla.

USING YOUR STAND MIXER, add butter cubes to dry mixture and stir together on low for 1–2 minutes. Butter will be in small, pea-sized pieces. Gradually add milk and egg mixture until batter comes together.

POUR BATTER into two 9-inch cake pans, lined with parchment paper and lightly greased. Bake at 350 degrees for 24–28 minutes until toothpick comes out clean. Remove from the oven and cool completely.

PREPARE YOUR CAKE by cutting the rounded tops off the cake layers (p. xv). Spread half the lemon curd on top of each layer before frosting the cake with the Stiff Whipped Cream. Then top with sliced strawberries. Garnish with more fresh strawberries, cool in refrigerator.

Lemon Curd

¾ cup sugar

3 eggs

¼ cup butter

½ cup lemon juice (fresh is always best, but not necessary)
1 lemon, zested (about 2 Tbsp.)

IN A SMALL SAUCEPAN, whisk together sugar and eggs. Then add butter, lemon juice, and lemon zest. Heat over medium for 8–10 minutes, until sauce starts to thicken and come together; cool completely.

Lemon Blueberry
Cake

Lemon Blueberry Cake

I had a request from my nephew to make his wedding cake and cupcakes. His bride wanted a blueberry cake with lemon frosting, and that is where this cake came from. It was a hit at the wedding. It's a classic.

3 cups flour

1½ cups sugar

1 Tbsp. baking powder

1 tsp. baking soda

pinch of salt

4 eggs

1 cup vegetable oil or grapeseed oil

¾ cup pureed fresh blueberries

½ cup freeze-dried blueberry crumbles

1 Tbsp. lemon zest

½ cup buttermilk

MIX TOGETHER flour, sugar, baking powder, soda, and salt. Set aside. In a separate bowl, combine eggs, oil, blueberries—both fresh and freeze-dried lemon zest, and buttermilk. Stir until combined.

ADD DRY INGREDIENTS to the wet and stir until mixture is combined. Pour into two 9-inch cake pans, lined with parchment paper and lightly greased. Bake at 350 degrees for 25–28 minutes until cake is golden and a toothpick comes out clean.

REMOVE FROM THE OVEN and cool completely. Frost cooled cake on middle, sides, and tops with Lemon Buttercream frosting (p.130).

Lemon Poke Cake

This vanilla cake is just wonderful with a little bit of lemon gelatin. It's perfection.

2½ cups flour

3 tsp. baking powder

1 tsp. baking soda

1¼ cups sugar

pinch of Kosher salt

3 eggs, room temperature

1 cup milk, room temperature

2 tsp. almond extract

1 tsp. vanilla bean paste (or vanilla extract)

¾ cup butter, softened and cut into cubes

1 recipe Stiff Whipped Cream (p. 124)

1 (4-oz.) pkg. lemon gelatin

IN A MEDIUM BOWL, combine flour, baking powder, baking soda, sugar, and salt. Stir to combine.

IN A SEPARATE BOWL, combine eggs and milk; break each egg, stirring to combine. Add almond extract and vanilla.

USING YOUR STAND MIXER, combine butter and dry mixture and stir together on low for 1–2 minutes. Butter will be in small pea-sized pieces. Gradually add milk and egg mixture until batter comes together.

POUR BATTER into a 9 x 13-inch cake pan, lightly greased. Bake at 350 degrees for 24–28 minutes until toothpick comes out clean. Remove from the oven and cool slightly. While still slightly warm, poke holes in the cake with a straw.

POUR LEMON GELATIN over top of cake evenly. Refrigerate 2–3 hours until gelatin is set. Top with Stiff Whipped Cream and grated lemon zest for garnish, if desired.

Banana Skillet Cake

This recipe was given to my mom from Aunt Kathy. You see, I come from a long line of great bakers. I am proud of my heritage. And I'm proud of how good this cake is. It has a perfect banana flavor and moist texture, and I could even eat this cake for breakfast.

1 cup flour

1 tsp. baking powder

½ tsp. baking soda

pinch of salt

½ cup butter

¾ cup sugar

3 medium ripe bananas, mashed

½ cup buttermilk

1 egg

1 tsp. vanilla extract

TOPPING:

½ cup butter, softened

½ cup brown sugar

½ cup flour

1 tsp. cinnamon

IN A MEDIUM BOWL, mix together flour, baking powder soda, and salt; set aside.

CREAM TOGETHER butter and sugar until light and fluffy, about 1–2 minutes. Add mashed bananas, buttermilk, egg, and vanilla extract. Stir until just combined. Pour into a greased 10-inch cast iron skillet.

THEN MAKE the topping. Using a pastry knife, cut together butter, brown sugar, flour, and cinnamon. Top batter with crumb topping and bake at 350 degrees for 25–28 minutes. Remove from the oven and cool completely.

Banana Skillet Cake

New York Cheesecake

I love to make any good food in the kitchen. I also love to eat out, mostly because it gives me a break from cooking, not to mention the cleanup. I also love to reverse-write recipes, and I have been working on a great cheesecake for longer than I can remember. This recipe has been worked through many, many times, and I dare say I think I nailed it.

3 (8-oz.) pkg. cream cheese (low-fat is okay), softened
3 eggs
3 heaping Tbsp. cornstarch
1 cup sugar
½ cup sour cream
¼ cup heavy cream
1 tsp. vanilla extract
juice of 1 Meyer lemon (or regular lemon)
CRUST:
2 cups graham cracker crumbs
¼ cup sugar
½ cup butter, melted

STIR TOGETHER crust ingredients to form a thick paste-like mixture. Place in the bottom of a 9-inch springform pan, pressing down to form crust. Bake in a preheated oven at 475 degrees for 5 minutes. Remove from the oven and set aside.

MEANWHILE, cream together cream cheese until smooth, scraping down the sides of the bowl. Add one egg at a time until blended. Slowly add sugar and sour cream. While the mixer is on low speed, add heavy cream and vanilla. Beat on medium speed for 2–3 minutes until batter is light and fluffy. Add lemon juice and beat until combined.

POUR BATTER onto partially cooked crust. Place the springform pan in a water bath and bake at 475 degrees for 8 minutes. Then reduce the heat to 350 degrees and bake for 35–40 minutes until cheesecake is golden brown on top and set. Do not open the oven. Turn off the heat and let cheesecake sit in the oven for 30 minutes.

REMOVE from the oven and let stand on the counter until room temperature. Place in the fridge for at least 6 hours before cutting for best results.

NEW YORK CHEESE-CAKE VARIATIONS:

Red Velvet Cheesecake

Red velvet is a decadent treat, worthy of any royalty.

MAKE NEW YORK CHEESECAKE according to directions. Before baking, add to batter:

½ cup cocoa

3 Tbsp. red velvet baking emulsion

CREAM until ingredients are combined and smooth. Bake according to directions. Top with whipped cream and a dusting of cocoa if desired.

Key Lime Cheesecake

You had me at Key lime. This cheesecake is my husband's absolute favorite dessert in the entire world. In fact, I could probably get anything I wanted if I made it for him. "Hey, honey, I made you some Key lime Cheesecake—I'm going to Hawaii for a week. Good luck with the kids!"

MAKE NEW YORK CHEESECAKE according to directions. Bake cheesecake. Then make Key Lime Curd.

Key Lime Curd:

¾ cup sugar

3 eggs

¼ cup butter

½ cup Key lime juice (fresh is best, but not necessary)

1 lime, zested (about 2 Tbsp.)

IN A SMALL SAUCEPAN, whisk together sugar and eggs. Then add butter, lime juice, and lime zest. Heat over medium until sauce starts to thicken and come together for 8–10 minutes, then cool completely. Spread cooled Key Lime Curd on top of cooled cheesecake before cutting.

HINT: Add ½ cup roasted Macadamia nuts to crust.

Nanaimo Cheesecake

If I could only have one treat for the rest of my life, it might just be this Nanaimo Cheesecake.

MAKE NEW YORK CHEESECAKE according to directions.

ADD TO CRUST:

½ cup roasted almonds

⅓ cup cocoa

½ cup sweetened shredded coconut

PULSE until combined. Bake according to directions.

BEFORE BAKING, add to batter:

3 Tbsp. Bird's Custard Powder (available online)

ONCE CHEESECAKE has cooled, heat ½ cup semi-sweet chocolate and 2 tablespoons butter together for 30 seconds on low in the microwave. Stir to combine. Allow to set and cool slightly. Spread over cooled cheesecake just before serving. Chocolate will harden in the fridge.

Chocolate Peanut Butter Cup a.k.a. Addison's Cheesecake

I may have outdone myself. This creamy texture with peanut butter and a touch of chocolate is a serious dessert for chocolate and peanut butter lovers.

MAKE NEW YORK CHEESECAKE according to directions. Before baking add:

1¼ cups creamy peanut butter

OMIT SOUR CREAM and lemon juice

STIR TO COMBINE and bake for 60 minutes. Cool. Top with 1 recipe Chocolate Ganache (p.134) and cut or chopped Chocolate Peanut Butter Cups (about 10 peanut butter cups).

Marissa's Pumpkin Spice Cheesecake

You can't go into the fall season without making a pumpkin cheesecake. It's the perfect blend of spices and pumpkin—together in a cheesecake. Oh. My.

MAKE NEW YORK CHEESECAKE according to directions. Before baking add:

1 cup pureed pumpkin, canned or fresh

1 Tbsp. Wise Woman of the East, or pumpkin pie spice

STIR TO COMBINE and bake for 60 to 65 minutes or until cake has set. Cool. Top with Stiff Whipped Cream (p.124) and caramel sauce if desired.

White Chocolate Raspberry Cheesecake

I first tried this kind of cheesecake at a local restaurant. It quickly became a favorite of mine, and I decided I needed to be able to make it in my own kitchen.

MAKE NEW YORK CHEESECAKE according to directions. Before baking add:

½ cup freeze-dried raspberry crumbles (available at food storage stores)
½ cup white chocolate, melted and cooled

STIR TO COMBINE and bake according to directions. Cool. Top with Stiff Whipped Cream (p.124) and Raspberry Glaze (p.133).

Dark Chocolate Cheesecake

I love chocolate. Anything chocolate. Especially dark chocolate. And together with cheesecake, I think this is pure heaven in a dessert.

MAKE NEW YORK CHEESECAKE according to directions. Before baking add:

½ cup dark chocolate cocoa powder

STIR TO COMBINE and bake according to directions. Cool. Top with Stiff Whipped Cream (p.124) or fresh berries and fresh whipped cream if desired for garnish.

Strawberry Cream Puff Cake

Not only is this cake impressive, it's also pretty easy to make. I loved putting the final touches on this cake, seeing it come to life. It was the highlight of the birthday party I made it for! Clearly, this cake is a keeper.

4 cups flour

2 cups sugar

1 tsp. baking soda

1 tsp. baking powder

½ cup cold butter, cut into small pieces

4 eggs

1 Tbsp. vanilla extract

1¼ cups milk

whole strawberries

30 small cream puffs

1 recipe Stiff Whipped Cream (p.124)

1 recipe Chocolate Ganache (p. 134)

MIX TOGETHER flour, sugar, baking soda, and baking powder. Cut butter pieces into flour mixture with a pastry cutter. Once butter is pea-sized, add eggs, vanilla, and milk.

POUR CAKE BATTER into two 10-inch round cake pans, greased, floured, and lined with parchment paper. Bake at 350 degrees for 25–28 minutes. Remove from the oven and cool completely. Slice cake into halves, preparing for layering with Stiff Whipped Cream. Place small cream puffs around the base of the layered cake; on the top layer, alternate strawberries and cream puffs. Drizzle with Chocolate Ganache.

Strawberry-
Cream Puff Cake

Yogurt Strawberry Bundt Cake

This tangy sweet strawberry cake calls my name, especially when strawberries are in season. It's a great cake for any reason, when you just want a light and refreshing cake.

1 cup butter, softened

1½ cups sugar

1 tsp. vanilla extract

5 oz. plain Greek yogurt

4 eggs

2¾ cups flour

1 tsp. baking soda

zest and juice of 1 lemon

2 cups diced strawberries

½ tsp. balsamic vinegar

pinch of salt

CREAM TOGETHER butter and sugar until light and fluffy for 1–2 minutes on medium speed. Add vanilla and yogurt, and mix until gently combined. Add 1 egg at a time until combined. In a separate bowl, mix together 2½ cups flour and baking soda. Gently add lemon juice and zest to the wet mixture until combined. Do not overmix.

GENTLY TOSS diced strawberries with remaining ¼ cup flour and add to cake batter.

POUR INTO a greased and floured 10-inch Bundt cake pan. Bake at 325 degrees for about 55–60 minutes or until cake is slightly browned and a toothpick comes out clean.

REMOVE FROM THE OVEN and cool. Top with Almond Glaze (p.131) if desired.

Creamy Lemon and Raspberry Chiffon

This cake has a light and airy texture that's worthy of a blue ribbon. It's full of lemon flavor, and if you use Meyer lemons, it becomes even better! Meyer lemons are amazing. I'm loving my lemon tree—who knew you could grow one in Utah?

7 eggs, separated, at room temperature

2 cups flour

1¼ cup sugar

3 tsp. baking powder

1 tsp. cream of tartar

2 Tbsp. grated lemon peel

2 tsp. lemon extract

½ cup vegetable oil

¾ cup water

pinch of salt

fresh raspberries and lemon zest for garnish

PREHEAT the oven to 325 degrees.

SIFT TOGETHER flour, sugar, baking powder, and cream of tartar. Add the lemon peel, and set aside. In a separate bowl, combine egg yolks, lemon extract, vegetable oil, water, and salt. Add dry mixture to wet. Batter will be a little thicker.

WITH A CLEAN BOWL AND A WHISK, whisk together egg whites until stiff peaks form. Gently fold egg whites into cake batter by thirds.

POUR BATTER into two lightly greased and parchment-lined 9-inch cake pans. Bake for 26–28 minutes or until cake springs back and is lightly golden. Invert cake pans onto a cooling rack and remove pans after 10 minutes. Cool cake completely before frosting with Lemon Glaze (p.46). Top with grated lemon zest and fresh raspberries.

Piña Colada Cake

It's five o'clock somewhere, isn't it? Thank goodness.

2½ cups flour

3 tsp. baking powder

1 tsp. baking soda

1¼ cups sugar

pinch of Kosher salt

3 eggs, room temperature

1 cup coconut milk, room temperature

2 tsp. coconut extract

1 tsp. vanilla bean paste (or vanilla extract)

¾ cup butter, softened and cut into cubes

1 cup shredded coconut

1 recipe Swiss Buttercream (p.135)

2 tsp. coconut extract

1 (8-oz.) can crushed pineapple, juice separated

½ cup chopped roasted pecans

maraschino cherries (optional)

IN A MEDIUM BOWL, combine flour, baking powder, baking soda, sugar, and salt. Stir to combine.

IN A SEPARATE BOWL, combine eggs and coconut milk and break each egg yolk, stirring to combine. Add coconut extract and vanilla.

USING YOUR STAND MIXER, combine butter and dry mixture and stir together on low for 1–2 minutes. Butter will be in small pea-sized pieces. Gradually add coconut milk and egg mixture until batter comes together. Add shredded coconut. Stir to combine.

POUR BATTER into two 9-inch cake pans, lined with parchment paper and lightly greased. Bake at 350 degrees for 24–28 minutes until toothpick comes out clean. Remove from the oven and cool completely.

WHIP COCONUT EXTRACT with finished Swiss Buttercream. Set aside. Divide Swiss Buttercream in half. Add pineapple chunks to half the cream and stir. Set aside. Brush cake layers with remaining pineapple juice. Top layers with pineapple cream mixture. Frost sides of cake with Stiff Whipped Cream.

TOP WITH CHOPPED PECANS and some maraschino cherries for garnish if desired.

Mango Mousse Cake

This cake reminds me of a tropical paradise where mangos are abundant and available on every corner. I love this cake for its sweet and creamy texture. Love. Love. Love.

2½ cups flour

3 tsp. baking powder

1 tsp. baking soda

1¼ cups sugar

pinch of Kosher salt

3 eggs, room temperature

1 cup milk, room temperature

2 tsp. almond extract

1 tsp. vanilla bean paste (or vanilla extract)

¾ cup butter, softened and cut into cubes

1 recipe Mango Sauce

1 recipe Stiff Whipped Cream (p.124)

IN A MEDIUM BOWL, combine flour, baking powder, baking soda, sugar, and salt. Stir to combine. In a separate bowl, combine eggs and milk and break each egg yolk, stirring to combine. Add almond extract and vanilla.

USING YOUR STAND MIXER, combine butter and dry mixture and stir together on low for 1–2 minutes. Butter will be in small pea-sized pieces. Gradually add milk and egg mixture until batter comes together.

POUR BATTER into two 9-inch cake pans, lined with parchment paper and lightly greased. Bake at 350 degrees for 24–28 minutes until toothpick comes out clean. Remove from the oven and cool completely.

PREPARE YOUR CAKE by cutting the rounded top off each cake layer (optional). Spread half of mango sauce on top of each layer before the Stiff Whipped Cream. Frost all sides, middle, and top with Stiff Whipped Cream, making a ridge around the top edge. Place remaining Mango Sauce on top of whipped cream to garnish.

Mango Sauce

¾ cup sugar

3 eggs

¼ cup butter

¾ cup mango puree (about 2 fresh mangos, peeled and pureed—fresh is best, but not necessary)

1 lemon, zested (about 2 Tbsp.)

IN A SMALL SAUCEPAN, whisk together sugar and eggs. Then add the butter, pureed mango, and lemon zest. Heat over medium for 8–10 minutes until sauce starts to thicken and come together, then cool completely.

Key Lime Pie Bundt Cake

I wish I could eat this cake for dessert every night. Every night! But that would be wrong. It's a show-stopper, both pretty and tasty. I love this cake.

1 cup butter, softened

1½ cups sugar

1 tsp. vanilla extract

5 oz. sour cream

4 eggs

1½ cups Key lime juice, divided

1 (10-oz.) can sweetened condensed milk

2¾ cups flour

1 tsp. baking soda

pinch of salt

GLAZE:

2 cups powdered sugar

1 Tbsp. heavy cream

1 Tbsp. Key lime juice

1–2 drops green food coloring (optional)

graham cracker crumbs

CREAM TOGETHER butter and sugar until light and fluffy for 1–2 minutes on medium speed. Add vanilla and sour cream and mix until gently combined. Add one egg at a time until combined. In a separate bowl, mix together 2½ cups flour and baking soda. Gently add ½ cup of lime juice to the wet mixture until combined. Do not overmix.

IN A SEPARATE BOWL, combine remaining 1 cup Key lime juice and sweetened condensed milk. Set aside.

POUR ¾ OF CAKE BATTER into a greased and floured 10-inch Bundt cake pan. Then, using a spoon, make a groove in center of batter, pour in sweetened condensed milk mixture, and cover with remaining batter. Bake at 325 degrees for about 35–40 minutes or until cake is slightly browned and a toothpick comes out clean.

REMOVE FROM THE OVEN and cool. Set cake upside-down to cool. Take cake out of the form, gently tapping the mold on the counter to loosen. Whisk glaze together: powdered sugar, cream, and Key lime juice. Add more cream to get desired consistency. Pour over cake and sprinkle with graham cracker crumbs.

Large Crumb Coffee Cake

There's never a wrong time to make or eat coffee cake. This cake is perfect for a brunch, or any party, really. It's addictive, that's for sure.

3 cups flour

1⅔ cups sugar

pinch of salt

2 Tbsp. baking powder

¾ cup vegetable oil

¾ cup milk

4 eggs

CRUMB:

1 cup brown sugar

2 Tbsp. cinnamon or Wise Woman of the East (www.honeyvillefarms.com)

1 cup vegetable shortening

2½ cups flour

pinch of salt

2 Tbsp. milk

4 Tbsp. butter, softened

MIX TOGETHER flour, sugar, salt, and baking powder. In a separate bowl, combine oil, milk, and eggs and whisk until combined. Slowly add dry ingredients, and stir until there are few or no lumps in the batter.

POUR BATTER into a 9 x 13-inch greased and floured baking sheet. In a mixer combine all crumb ingredients. The crumb mixture should be soft, but not dry. Place crumbles on top of batter.

BAKE AT 350 DEGREES for 25–30 minutes or until light golden brown. Let cool for 15 minutes and dust with powdered sugar.

Almond Raspberry Texas Sheet Cake

This cake is a variation of your traditional Texas Sheet Cake. It's fresh and amazing cake, and topping it with raspberries really makes the cake!

1 cup water

1 cup butter

½ cup sugar

2 cups flour

2 eggs

1 tsp. almond emulsion or pure extract

½ cup sour cream

1 tsp. baking soda

fresh raspberries for garnish

1 (16-oz.) can raspberry pie filling

1 recipe Almond Glaze (p.131)

BRING TO A BOIL water and butter in a small saucepan. Once butter has melted, remove from the heat and cool slightly. Add sugar and flour, and stir. Combine remaining ingredients until smooth.

POUR BATTER into a greased 10 x 15-inch jelly roll pan, and bake at 350 degrees for 20–22 minutes. Top with raspberry pie filling, Almond Glaze, and fresh raspberries.

Almond Raspberry
Texas Sheet Cake

Luau (Passion Fruit) Cake

There's a pattern emerging in this cake book. A lot of tropical flavoring in cakes. And why not? It's a great pairing for a dessert—especially in summertime.

4 cups flour

2 cups sugar

1 tsp. baking soda

1 tsp. baking powder

½ cup cold butter, cut into small pieces

4 eggs

1 tsp. vanilla extract

1¼ cup milk

MIX TOGETHER flour, sugar, baking soda, and baking powder. Cut butter pieces into flour mixture with a pastry cutter. Once butter is pea-sized, add eggs, vanilla, and milk.

POUR CAKE BATTER into two 10-inch round cake pans, greased, floured, and lined with parchment paper. Bake at 350 degrees for 25–28 minutes. Remove from the oven and cool completely. Slice cake into halves horizontally, preparing for layering with passion fruit filling. Frost with Stiff Whipped Cream (p.124).

Passion Fruit Filling

¾ cup sugar

¼ cup cornstarch

1 cup passion fruit nectar or puree

4 egg yolks

1 tsp. vanilla extract

1 stick unsalted butter, cut into tablespoons

WHISK TOGETHER sugar and cornstarch in a medium saucepan. Add passion fruit nectar, egg yolks, and vanilla. Whisk for 4–5 minutes over medium heat until sauce thickens. Remove from the heat and stir in butter, one tablespoon at a time. Cover filling with plastic wrap, allowing wrap to touch top of filling. Refrigerate for at least 2 hours before use.

Southern Apple Cake with Butterscotch Sauce

This is a southern classic apple cake, and it is made even more special with this butterscotch sauce.

1⅓ cups vegetable oil

1½ cups sugar

3 eggs

2¾ cups whole wheat flour ·

1 Tbsp. cinnamon

1 tsp. salt

1 tsp. baking soda

3–4 Granny Smith apples, chopped with skins

1 tsp. vanilla

1 recipe Butterscotch Sauce (pg. 139)

BEAT OIL, SUGAR, AND EGGS for 3–4 minutes until light and fluffy. Add dry ingredients and beat on low until combined. Add apple chunks and the batter will moisten. Add vanilla and mix all until combined. Pour into a 12-cup Bundt pan that has been buttered and floured.

BAKE AT 350 DEGREES for 1 hour and 20 minutes, or until a toothpick comes out clean. .

Butterscotch Sauce

½ cup butter

1 cup brown sugar

¼ cup evaporated milk

pinch of salt

1 tsp. vanilla

COOK 5–7 minutes. Pour sauce over warm cake before serving.

Apple Pie Sheet Cake with Maple Glaze

To me, one of the best flavors of fall is apple pie. So how about an apple pie cake? Sounds good to me!

1¾ cups sugar

1 cup unsalted butter

1 tsp. vanilla

4 eggs

3 cups flour

1½ tsp. baking powder

1 tsp. cinnamon

2 (21-oz.) cans apple pie filling

1 recipe Maple Glaze (p.129)

CREAM together sugar and butter. Then add vanilla and eggs. Combine the flour, baking powder and cinnamon and add to creamed mixture.

SPREAD TWO-THIRDS OF THE MIXTURE on the bottom of the greased 9 x 13-inch cake pan or jelly roll pan. Spread the pie filling on top. Drop the remaining dough on top. Bake at 350 degrees for 30–35 minutes. Top with Maple Glaze while still warm.

Apple Pie
Sheet Cake

Cherry Almond Sheet Cake with Almond Glaze

I first had this cake at a family party years and years ago. Here's my version; it's simple and yummy. Simple is the best.

1 ¾ cups sugar

1 cup unsalted butter

1 tsp. vanilla

4 eggs

3 cups flour

1 ½ tsp. baking powder

2 (21-oz.) cans cherry pie filling

1 recipe Almond Glaze (p.131)

CREAM TOGETHER sugar and butter. Then add vanilla and eggs. Combine flour and baking powder and add to creamed mixture. Spread two-thirds of mixture in greased 9 x 13-inch cake pan or jelly roll pan. Spread pie filling on top. Drop remaining dough on top. Bake at 350 degrees for 30–35 minutes. Top with Almond Glaze while still warm.

Carrot Cake

I received this recipe years ago and still make it for special occasions. You can omit the nuts or raisins to make this cake special for your family. I sometimes think carrot cake should count as a vegetable. Wait. Do you ever think of things like that, or is it just me?

3 cups flour

2 cups sugar

½ tsp. salt

2 tsp. baking soda

I tsp. cinnamon

I tsp. vanilla

¾ cup vegetable oil

3 eggs

½ cup shredded coconut (optional)

I cup chopped nuts

I cup raisins

1½ cups water

I small can crushed pineapple with juice

Cream Cheese Buttercream (p.138)

MIX TOGETHER all dry ingredients: flour, sugar, salt, baking soda, and cinnamon. Boil raisins with water. Let stand for 5 minutes. In a separate bowl, mix, oil, carrots, eggs, vanilla, then add all wet ingredients together and stir. Slowly add dry ingredients, I cup at a time, until incorporated.

POUR INTO two 9-inch cake pans, lined with parchment paper and lightly greased. Bake at 350 for 50–60 minutes or until a toothpick comes out clean. Cool completely. Frost sides, middle and top with Cream Cheese Buttercream.

Italian Lemon Cream Cake

A while back I had the privilege to go to New York on a business trip. My husband and I went to Little Italy and we had a slice of this cake for dessert. Each bite was a little bit of heaven.

CAKE:

2¼ cups flour

1 cup sugar

4 egg whites

½ cup butter, softened

1 tsp. vanilla extract

3 tsp. baking powder

pinch of salt

1 cup buttermilk

SIMPLE SYRUP:

½ cup sugar

½ cup water

2 Tbsp. lemon juice

FILLING/FROSTING:

1 cup Lemon Curd (p. 5) or pie filling

4 oz. cream cheese, softened

1 cup heavy cream

1 Tbsp. lemon juice

CRUMB TOPPING:

½ cup flour

½ cup powdered sugar

1 tsp. vanilla extract

⅓ cup cold unsalted butter, cut into small pieces

CAKE: Cream together butter and sugar. Add vanilla and egg whites. Gently add flour and baking powder. Then add buttermilk, 2 tablespoons at a time until combined. Pour cake batter into a 9-inch greased and parchment-lined round cake pan.

BAKE AT 350 for 25–28 minutes. Remove from the oven and cool.

SIMPLE SYRUP: Over medium heat in a small saucepan, stir sugar, water, and lemon juice until sugar is completely dissolved. About 4–6 minutes. Set aside to cool.

FILLING/FROSTING: Cream together lemon curd, cream cheese, and heavy cream until light and fluffy. Add lemon zest.

CRUMB TOPPING: Using a pastry cutter, cut flour, powdered sugar, vanilla extract, and butter into tiny pieces, pea-sized is best. Set aside.

TO CONSTRUCT THE CAKE: cut cake in half evenly. Place bottom of cake on serving dish, then brush top with simple syrup, generously. Top with ⅓ of the filling. Spread to ½-inch from sides. Place remaining cake, dome side up, onto middle layer of frosting. Top with more frosting mixture and frost sides with remaining frosting. Top both sides and top of cake with crumb mixture.

REFRIGERATE until ready to serve.

Peaches and Cream Pound Cake

Pound cake has its name for a reason. Usually, this cake has a pound of butter. And when I say butter, I mean butter. Most of the time, more is better. And if someone tells you otherwise, it's obvious that you don't need that negativity in your life.

½ lb. butter, softened

½ lb. vegetable shortening

2½ cups sugar

pinch of salt

½ tsp. baking soda

6 eggs

¾ cup milk

1 tsp. vanilla extract

3 cups flour

1 recipe Stiff Whipped Cream (p.124)

2–3 cups sliced fresh peaches, sweetened with sugar (1–2 Tbsp.) if needed

CREAM TOGETHER butter, shortening, sugar, salt, and baking soda. Add eggs one at a time. Then add milk and vanilla extract. Add flour and gently mix until just combined. Do not overmix batter. Pour into a greased and floured 10-inch Bundt pan.

BAKE THE CAKE at 350 degrees for 60–90 minutes, until cake springs back when lightly touched and top is golden brown.

Peaches and Cream Pound Cake

Zesty Lemon Petite Fours

Holy cow. I have no words for how good these little cakes are. They are simply darling. And stunning. And perfect for a good friend's birthday party.

1½ cups flour

1¼ cups sugar, divided

7 eggs, separated, at room temperature

pinch of salt

2 medium lemons, zested and juiced

¼ cup lime juice

1½ tsp. vanilla extract

1 tsp. cream of tartar

1 cup Lemon Curd recipe (p.5)

LEMON GLAZE:

2½ cups powdered sugar

2–3 Tbsp. lemon juice

IN A LARGE BOWL mix together flour, 1 cup sugar, egg yolks, salt, zest and juice of lemons, lime juice, vanilla, and cream of tartar. Batter will be very sticky. Set aside.

IN A SEPARATE BOWL, whisk egg whites until stiff peaks form, 1–2 minutes. Gradually add remaining ¼ cup sugar and keep mixing until egg whites become glossy, about another minute.

FOLD ONE-FOURTH OF EGG WHITE MIXTURE into thick batter gently. Then add another one-fourth of egg whites until cake batter becomes even more light. Then add final egg whites until batter is light and fluffy.

POUR INTO 10 x 15 x 1-inch parchment-lined jelly pan roll. Bake at 325 degrees for 27–29 minutes. Remove from the oven and cool completely.

ONCE CAKE IS COOL, use a small cookie cutter with about 2-inch diameter to cut small circles out of cooled cake. Place cookie cutter as close together as possible. Getting about 20–22 small rounds.

PLACE ONE ROUND on a wire rack, topping with a dollop of Lemon Curd. Place a second round on top, slightly pressing down. Using a knife, scrape any excess Lemon Curd away from cake. Whisk together remaining powdered sugar and lemon juice to make glaze. Whisk until no more clumps remain. Drizzle finished cakes with glaze and let set for 10–20 minutes.

TOP SMALL GLAZED CAKES with crushed lemon candies, lemon zest, or yellow sprinkles for garnish if desired, before glaze sets.

MAKES ABOUT 10 SERVINGS.

Angel Food Cake

Angel food cake is a great way to finish off a meal. To make it even more gourmet, I'd pair it with some fresh fruit or berries and cream to really top it all off.

1 dozen large eggs, separated and at room temperature

1½ cups sugar

1 cup flour

1 tsp. cream of tartar

pinch of salt

1 lemon, juiced

1 tsp. vanilla extract

PREHEAT the oven to 350 degrees.

WHISK TOGETHER EGG WHITES until soft peaks form. Add cream of tartar and ½ cup of sugar and continue mixing until stiff peaks form, about 2 more minutes. In a separate bowl, combine the remaining sugar and flour. With a spoon, bring both together to mix. Once egg whites are stiff, gently fold together half of sugar and flour mixture with egg whites. Then continue to add remaining mixture. Gently fold in lemon juice and vanilla extract.

POUR BATTER into at 10-inch tube pan that has been greased and floured. Bake at 350 degrees for 35–40 minutes. Remove from the oven and invert on a wire rack to cool.

TOP with Stiff Whipped Cream (p.124) and fresh berries if desired.

Angel Food Cake

Orange and Olive Oil Cake

Orange and Olive Oil Cake

Here's something a little more healthy, but full of flavor. This cake is delicious with fresh fruit and whipped cream on the side.

2½ cups flour

1 cup sugar

zest of 2 medium oranges

1 tsp. orange extract

½ cup extra virgin olive oil or orange flavored olive oil

½ cup buttermilk

3 eggs

3 tsp. baking powder

pinch of salt

COMBINE FLOUR AND SUGAR in a medium bowl. In a separate bowl, combine orange zest, extract, olive oil, buttermilk, and eggs. Stir to combine, then add dry ingredients. Add baking powder and salt. Gently fold batter until combined, being careful not to overmix.

POUR INTO two 9-inch greased and parchment-lined round cake pans. Bake at 250 degrees for 22–25 minutes. Cake will be slightly golden.

REMOVE FROM THE OVEN and cool completely before frosting. Top with Stiff Whipped Cream (p.124) or fresh berries for garnish.

The Sweetness of Chocolate

Chocolate Raspberry-
Flourless Cake

Chocolate Raspberry Flourless Cake

This recipe is for Kerry. May you always have your cake and be able to eat it too!

1 (12-oz.) pkg. dark chocolate chips

¼ cup dark cocoa

1 tsp. vanilla bean paste or pure vanilla extract

1 cup brown sugar

1 cup heavy cream

6 eggs

fresh raspberries

½ recipe Chocolate Ganache (p.134)

HEAT the heavy cream and pour over the dark chocolate chips. Let stand for 2 minutes.

ADD DARK COCOA, vanilla, and brown sugar. Then gently add eggs, one at a time, until cake batter is nice and smooth. Butter a 9-inch springform pan and cover bottom with aluminum foil to prevent leaking. Pour batter into pan and place in steam bath to bake at 325 degrees for 40–42 minutes. Cool completely. Top with Chocolate Ganache and fresh raspberries.

Chocolate Mint Ice Cream Roll

This cake is impressive yet easy to assemble. Don't let the steps fool you. And the best part? You can make it a week in advance.

½ cup flour

½ cup cocoa

½ tsp. baking powder

5 eggs

½ cup sugar

1 tsp. vanilla extract

1½ quarts mint chocolate chip ice cream

1 recipe Chocolate Ganache (p.134)

½ tsp. mint extract or 2–3 drops peppermint essential oil

HEAT THE OVEN TO 375 DEGREES. Combine flour, cocoa, and baking powder. Separate egg white from egg yolks into 2 large bowls. Beat egg whites until soft and foamy. Add ¼ cup sugar. Continue to beat until egg whites become stiff. Set aside. Beat egg yolks and ¼ cup remaining sugar for about 2 minutes, until the egg yolks become thicker.

ADD FLOUR MIXTURE to egg yolks and ¼ of the egg whites mixture. Stir gently until combined. Gradually fold the remaining egg whites.

SPREAD BATTER into a greased and parchment-lined jelly roll pan. Don't skimp on the greasing.

BAKE for 12 minutes. Cake will spring back when lightly touched. Remove from the oven and cool about 5 minutes. Dust a cotton kitchen towel with powdered sugar. Invert cake onto dusted towel and remove parchment paper.

STARTING AT THE SHORTER END, roll warm cake in towel and let cool completely while still rolled up. (Keep the seam side down to hold the cake tight)

PLACE ICE CREAM on the counter and let soften while cake is cooling. When ice cream is soft, unroll cake and spread ice cream on top. Roll up again, tightly.

WRAP WITH PARCHMENT PAPER and seal again with aluminum foil. Freeze until solid for up to 1 week.

WHEN READY TO GLAZE with Ganache, mix peppermint extract or oil into frosting, remove cake from the wrapper, and place on a wire rack. Slice ends off clean. Drizzle with ganache and place back in the freezer for 20 minutes to set again. Slice into 1-inch slices for serving.

HINT: The best size jelly roll pan to use is 15 x 10 x 1-inch. If you want some variations, change the ice cream flavor!

Raspberry Chocolate Cake

This cake can be made with confidence. Confidence that those you are serving it to will believe you spent all day in the kitchen slaving away; when really, it will take hardly any time at all. That's the best way to bake.

3 cups flour

½ cup sugar

1 cup brown sugar

1 tsp baking soda

1 tsp. baking powder

¾ cup cocoa

pinch of salt

½ cup vegetable oil

1⅔ cups buttermilk

2 tsp. vanilla extract

½ recipe Fruit Buttercream (p.128) made with raspberries

½ recipe Chocolate Ganache (p.134)

fresh raspberries for garnish

IN A MEDIUM BOWL, mix together flour, sugars, baking soda, baking powder, cocoa, and salt. Stir until combined well. In a separate bowl, mix together vegetable oil, buttermilk, and vanilla extract.

ADD WET INGREDIENTS to dry mixture and stir until combined. Do not overmix. Pour batter equally into 3 greased and parchment-lined 9-inch pans. Bake at 350 degrees for 23–25 minutes, until cake springs back when lightly touched. Remove from the oven and cool completely.

CUT EACH COOLED LAYER in half horizontally. Layer cooled cake with Raspberry Buttercream frosting, leaving sides and top of cake free of frosting. Dust with powdered sugar, fresh raspberries, and a drizzle of Chocolate Ganache.

Chocolate Orange Cake

I don't know why, but when I taste chocolate and orange together, I think of Christmas.

3 cups flour

½ cup sugar

1 cup brown sugar

1 tsp. baking soda

1 tsp. baking powder

¾ cup cocoa

pinch of salt

½ cup vegetable oil

1⅔ cups buttermilk

2 tsp. orange extract

1 recipe Chocolate Buttercream (p.127)

2 cups orange marmalade, warmed

curled orange zest for garnish (optional)

IN A MEDIUM BOWL, mix together flour, sugars, baking soda, baking powder, cocoa, and salt. Stir until combined well. In a separate bowl, mix together vegetable oil, buttermilk, and vanilla extract.

ADD WET INGREDIENTS to dry mixture and stir until combined. Do not overmix. Pour batter equally into 3 greased and parchment-lined 9-inch cake pans. Bake at 350 degrees for 23–25 minutes, until cake springs back when lightly touched. Remove from the oven and cool completely.

CUT EACH CAKE LAYER in half horizontally. Cut rounded top off each cake off as well, making the cake even for stacking. Spread cooled layers with warmed marmalade, then frost with Chocolate Buttercream on both sides and top.

TOP with curled orange zest for garnish.

Chocolate Avocado Cake

Please, please, please make sure this cake is added to your menu. It is so rich and moist and has a perfect chocolate flavor.

2 cups flour

½ cup sugar

1 cup brown sugar

1 tsp. baking soda

1 tsp. baking powder

¾ cup cocoa

pinch of salt

1¼ cups buttermilk

2 eggs

1 medium avocado, ripe and mashed

2 tsp. vanilla extract

IN A MEDIUM BOWL, combine flour, sugars, baking soda, baking powder, cocoa, and salt. In a separate bowl, combine buttermilk, eggs, avocado, and vanilla extract. Then combine two bowls together until just combined.

POUR BATTER into two greased and parchment-lined 9-inch cake pans. Bake at 350 degrees for 20–22 minutes. Remove cake from the oven and cool completely. Frost with Chocolate Buttercream (p.127) or Chocolate Ganache (p.134).

Triple Chocolate Berry Cake

For this recipe I wanted the chocolate cake and berries to be the show. So I kept this cake clean, without frosting on the top and sides.

3 cups flour

½ cup sugar

I cup brown sugar

I tsp. baking soda

I tsp. baking powder

¾ cup cocoa

pinch of salt

½ cup vegetable oil

1⅔ cups buttermilk

2 tsp. vanilla extract

I recipe Vanilla Buttercream frosting (p.125)

I recipe Chocolate Ganache (p.134)

fresh or frozen blueberries, raspberries and blackberries

IN A MEDIUM BOWL, mix together flour, sugars, baking soda, baking powder, cocoa, and salt. Stir until well combined.

IN A SEPARATE BOWL, mix together vegetable oil, buttermilk, and vanilla extract. Add wet ingredients to dry mixture and stir until combined. Do not overmix. Pour batter into three greased and parchment-lined 9-inch cake pans. Bake at 350 degrees for 23–25 minutes, until cake springs back when lightly touched. Remove from the oven and cool completely.

CUT CAKE LAYERS to make them even (p. xv). Frost middle layers only, spreading fresh berries on top of each layer of frosting. Sprinkle powdered sugar and fresh berries on top for garnish.

Triple Chocolate-
Mousse Cake

Triple Chocolate Mousse Cake

I love getting ideas from friends, and I loved this idea. It turned out simply fantastic.

1 cup flour

1 cup dark brown sugar

½ cup cocoa

1 tsp baking powder

1 tsp. vanilla extract

2 eggs

½ cup milk

⅓ cup vegetable oil

½ recipe Chocolate Ganache (p.134)

1 recipe Stiff Whipped Cream (p.124), divided in half

1 (4-oz.) pkg. white chocolate instant pudding mix

chocolate shavings or curls for garnish

MIX TOGETHER flour, brown sugar, cocoa, baking powder, vanilla, eggs, milk, and oil. Batter will be thick. Pour batter into parchment-lined 10-inch springform pan. Bake at 350 degrees for 20–22 minutes. Remove from the oven and cool completely.

MEANWHILE, MIX CHOCOLATE GANACHE with half of Stiff Whipped Cream. Fold together and set aside. Then add remaining Stiff Whipped Cream to white chocolate instant pudding mix.

PREPARE CAKE by leveling it out, cutting rounded top off horizontally (p.xvi). Spread dark chocolate mousse evenly over cooled cake. Place in freezer for 20 minutes to set. Then top with white chocolate mousse topping. Place in freezer for 20 minutes to set. Top with chocolate shavings or curls.

Chocolate Cream Cake

This is one of my dad's favorite cakes, and he's more partial to pies. This cake has a perfect chocolate flavor and a creamy filling, topped with the best chocolate buttercream frosting. Need I say more?

2 cups flour

½ cup sugar

1 cup brown sugar

1 tsp. baking soda

1 tsp. baking powder

¾ cup cocoa

pinch of salt

½ cup vegetable oil

1¼ cups buttermilk

2 eggs

2 tsp. vanilla extract

1 recipe Stiff Whipped Cream (p.124)

1 recipe Chocolate Buttercream (p.127)

chocolate curls for garnish (optional)

IN A MEDIUM BOWL, mix together flour, sugars, baking soda, baking powder, cocoa, and salt. Stir until well combined. In a separate bowl, mix together vegetable oil, buttermilk, eggs, and vanilla extract. Add wet ingredients to dry mixture and stir until combined. Do not overmix. Pour batter into two greased and parchment-lined 9-inch cake pans. Bake at 350 degrees for 20–23 minutes, until cake springs back when lightly touched. Remove from the oven and cool completely.

SPREAD STIFF WHIPPED CREAM on the top of bottom cake layer. Then top with second cooled cake layer. Frost entire cake with Chocolate Buttercream (p.127).

TOP WITH CHOCOLATE CURLS for garnish (optional).

Chocolate Texas Sheet Cake

The BEST Texas sheet cake I've ever had, made, and drooled over. I love it so much. In fact, there are rarely any pieces left when I make this. Only crumbs.

1 cup butter

1 cup water

5 Tbsp. cocoa

2 cups flour

1½ cups brown sugar

pinch of salt

½ cup buttermilk

2 eggs

1 tsp. baking soda

1 tsp. vanilla extract

CHOCOLATE FROSTING:

½ cup butter

3 Tbsp. cocoa

3 Tbsp. milk

1 tsp. vanilla extract

1 lb. powdered sugar

½ cup chopped nuts (optional)

IN A MEDIUM SAUCEPAN, heat butter, water, and cocoa. Whisk until smooth and simmering. In a separate bowl, combine flour, sugar, and salt. Gently stir together. Add hot chocolate liquid and stir together. Then add buttermilk, eggs, baking soda, and vanilla once the batter has cooled slightly.

POUR into a greased 15 x 10 x 1-inch jelly roll pan. Bake at 350 degrees for 18–24 minutes, until cake springs back when lightly touched. Remove from the oven and cool for 10 minutes before frosting.

MEANWHILE, MAKE FROSTING. In a saucepan combine butter, cocoa, and milk and bring to a boil. Remove from heat and add vanilla and powdered sugar. Stir until smooth. Frost cake while warm.

Dark Chocolate Covered Strawberries

Chocolate covered strawberries are perfect for Valentine's Day or any day you want to celebrate those you love the most.

3 cups flour

½ cup sugar

1 cup brown sugar

1 tsp. baking soda

1 tsp. baking powder

¾ cup cocoa

pinch of salt

½ cup vegetable oil

1¼ cups buttermilk

3 eggs

2 tsp. vanilla extract

1 recipe Chocolate Swiss Buttercream (p.135)

1 recipe Chocolate Ganache (p.134)

1 pound whole large strawberries (10–13 medium strawberries to cover cake)

white melting chocolate

Valentine's Day themed colored sprinkles (optional)

IN A MEDIUM BOWL, mix together flour, sugars, baking soda, baking powder, cocoa, and salt. Stir until well combined.

IN A SEPARATE BOWL, mix together vegetable oil, buttermilk, eggs, and vanilla extract. Add wet ingredients to dry mixture and stir until combined. Do not overmix. Pour batter into two greased and parchment-lined 9-inch cake pans. Bake at 350 degrees for 20–23 minutes, until cake springs back when lightly touched. Remove from the oven and cool completely.

WASH AND DRY strawberries. Dip strawberries into warm chocolate ganache, gently tapping off excess chocolate, and place on a piece of wax or parchment paper to set. Sprinkle with Valentine's edible sprinkles if desired. Repeat until all strawberries are done. Set aside.

TO ASSEMBLE CAKE, place bottom layer on a cake plate, taking time to make sure top of cake is even (p.xv). Then frost middle layer with Chocolate Swiss Buttercream frosting. Then place final layer of cake on top of middle layer, making sure cake is even on top. Frost entire cake with remaining buttercream frosting.

TOP WITH CHOCOLATE COVERED STRAWBERRIES. Cool completely. Drizzle with white melting chocolate for garnish if desired.

Chocolate S'more Bundt Cake

S'mores aren't just for camping anymore. I believe you can eat them any time of the year. This cake is a good example of my quest to enjoy s'mores in my own home, anytime I want, without the mess of roasting marshmallows. This cake is a perfect and delicious way to do just that.

1 cup butter, softened

1½ cups sugar

1 tsp. vanilla extract

5 oz. sour cream

4 eggs

½ cup cocoa powder

2¾ cups flour, divided

1 tsp. baking soda

1 tsp. baking powder

pinch of salt

1 recipe Chocolate Ganache (p.134)

crushed Graham Crackers

½ cup chocolate chips

MARSHMALLOW GLAZE:

3 egg whites

pinch of salt

½ cup sugar

½ tsp. vanilla extract

CREAM TOGETHER butter and sugar until light and fluffy, 1–2 minutes at medium speed. Add vanilla and sour cream and mix until gently combined. Add one egg at a time until combined. In a separate bowl, mix together cocoa, flour, baking soda, baking powder, and salt. Do not overmix.

POUR CAKE BATTER into a greased and floured 10-inch Bundt cake pan. Bake at 325 degrees for about 35–40 minutes or until cake is slightly browned and a toothpick comes out clean.

REMOVE FROM THE OVEN and cool. Set cake upside down to cool. Take cake out of form, gently tapping mold on a counter to loosen.

WHILE CAKE IS COOLING, combine Marshmallow Glaze ingredients in a small saucepan. Whisk over medium heat for 4–6 minutes or until sugar is dissolved. Place marshmallow mixture in a mixer and beat at high speed until soft peaks form.

ADD VANILLA and fold together. Gently pour over cooled cake. Then drizzle as much of Ganache over top of marshmallow glaze. Top frosted cake with chocolate chips and sprinkle with graham cracker crumbs.

German Chocolate Cake

What a great cake. I always love making it and serving it to company. With the chewy coconut caramel topping, it's always a winner. If your family is like mine, they don't especially like nuts. I leave them out—putting them in the topping is optional.

3 cups flour

½ cup sugar

1 cup brown sugar

1 tsp. baking soda

1 tsp. baking powder

¾ cup cocoa

pinch of salt

½ cup vegetable oil

1⅔ cups buttermilk

2 tsp. vanilla extract

1 recipe Chocolate Buttercream (p.127)

1 recipe Coconut Caramel Topping (see opposite page)

IN A MEDIUM BOWL, mix together flour, sugars, baking soda, baking powder, cocoa, and salt. Stir until combined well.

IN A SEPARATE BOWL, mix together vegetable oil, buttermilk, and vanilla extract. Add wet ingredients to dry mixture and stir until combined. Do not overmix. Pour batter into greased and parchment-lined 9-inch cake pans. Bake at 350 degrees for 23–25 minutes, until cake springs back when lightly touched. Remove from the oven and cool completely. Frost sides and top with Chocolate Buttercream frosting and top with Coconut Caramel Topping.

COCONUT CARAMEL TOPPING:

2 cups shredded coconut

1 cup brown sugar

½ cup butter

½ cup heavy cream

pinch of salt

½ cup chopped pecans (optional)

IN A MEDIUM SAUCEPAN over medium heat, cook coconut, sugar, butter, and heavy cream until it reaches a low simmer. Cook for 2 minutes. Add salt and nuts. Remove from stove and cool completely before adding to top of cake.

Mounds of Joy Bundt Cake

Because sometimes you feel like a nut, and sometimes you really don't. Now you can choose what you're in the mood for. And either way, it's bound to be a joyful experience.

1 cup butter, softened

1½ cups sugar

1 tsp. vanilla extract

5 oz. sour cream

4 eggs

½ cup cocoa powder

2¾ cups flour

1 tsp. baking soda

1 tsp. baking powder

pinch of salt

COCONUT ALMOND FILLING:

2½ cups powdered sugar

1 (10-oz.) can sweetened condensed milk

1 tsp. coconut extract

1 cup shredded coconut

½ cup sliced almonds (optional)

pinch of salt

COCONUT GLAZE:

2 cups powdered sugar

pinch of salt

½ cup heavy cream

½ tsp. coconut extract

CREAM TOGETHER butter and sugar until light and fluffy, 1–2 minutes on medium speed. Add vanilla and sour cream and mix until gently combined. Add 1 egg at a time until combined. In a separate bowl, mix together cocoa, 2½ cups flour, baking soda, baking powder, and salt. Do not overmix. In a separate bowl, mix together coconut and almond filling. Mixture will be thick.

POUR CAKE BATTER into a greased and floured 10-inch Bundt cake pan. Then spoon coconut filling into middle of batter. Bake at 325 degrees for about 35–40 minutes or until cake is slightly browned and a toothpick comes out clean.

REMOVE FROM THE OVEN and cool. Set cake upside down to cool. Take cake out of form, gently tapping mold on kitchen counter to loosen. Mix together coconut glaze and pour over cooled Bundt cake. Sprinkle with coconut or both coconut and almonds for garnish.

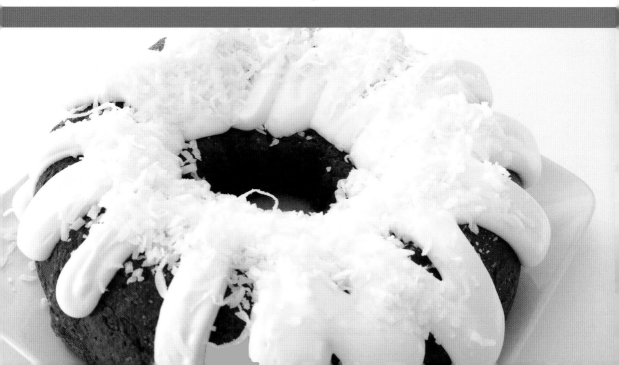

Chocolate Caramel Pretzel Cake

This recipe makes an amazing cupcake. It has caramel, chocolate, salt, and pretzels as its primary flavors. How could I not include a from-scratch recipe to convert this into a layered cake? I simply had to.

3 cups flour

½ cup sugar

1 cup brown sugar

1 tsp. baking soda

1 tsp. baking powder

¾ cup cocoa

pinch of salt

½ cup vegetable oil

1⅔ cups buttermilk

2 tsp. vanilla extract

1 recipe Chocolate Buttercream (p.127)

pretzels for garnish

Kosher salt

caramel sauce (I love Mrs. Richardson's Butterscotch sauce)

IN A MEDIUM BOWL, mix together flour, sugars, baking soda, baking powder, cocoa, and salt. Stir until well combined.

IN A SEPARATE BOWL, mix together vegetable oil, buttermilk, and vanilla extract. Add wet ingredients to dry mixture and stir until combined. Do not overmix. Pour batter into greased and parchment-lined

9-inch cake pans. Bake at 350 degrees for 23–25 minutes, until cake springs back when lightly touched. Remove from the oven and cool completely.

LAYER COOLED CAKE with Chocolate Buttercream frosting on sides, layered middle of cake, and top. Place pretzels around cake, pressing into fresh frosting to secure. Then drizzle caramel sauce and sprinkle with Kosher salt.

Mint Chocolate Chip Cake

What's your favorite ice cream flavor? One of my go-to flavors is mint chocolate chip. Now it's a cake. But don't let that stop you from adding a scoop of your favorite mint chocolate chip ice cream on top of your piece.

3 cups flour

½ cup sugar

I cup brown sugar

I tsp. baking soda

I tsp. baking powder

¾ cup cocoa

pinch of salt

½ cup vegetable oil

1⅔ cups buttermilk

2 tsp. vanilla extract

I tsp. peppermint extract

I recipe Vanilla Buttercream (p.125)

I cup mini chocolate chips

½ tsp. peppermint extract or peppermint oil

I tsp. green food coloring

IN A MEDIUM BOWL, mix together flour, sugars, baking soda, baking powder, cocoa, and salt. Stir until well combined. In a separate bowl, mix together vegetable oil, buttermilk, and vanilla extract. Add wet ingredients to dry mixture and stir until combined. Do not overmix. Pour batter into greased and parchment-lined 9-inch cake pans. Bake at 350 degrees for 23–25 minutes, until cake springs back when lightly touched. Remove from the oven and cool completely.

CREAM TOGETHER Vanilla Buttercream frosting, mini chocolate chips, mint extract, and food coloring. Frost layers, side, and top with mint chocolate chip frosting.

Layered Cookie Cake

I know that technically this is not a "cake," but it looks like a cake and it's a really fun way to celebrate.

1 cup butter, softened

¼ cup sugar

¾ cup brown sugar

1 tsp. vanilla

2 eggs

1 (4-oz.) pkg. vanilla instant pudding mix

1 tsp. baking soda

2¼ cups flour

2 cups semi-sweet chocolate chips

1 recipe Vanilla Buttercream frosting (p.125)

CREAM TOGETHER butter and sugars until light and fluffy. Add vanilla, eggs, and pudding mix (dry powder only). In a separate bowl, mix together baking soda and flour and gently add to wet ingredients. Fold in chocolate chips. Use a small cookie scoop to drop dough onto lightly greased cookie sheet. Bake at 350 degrees for 8–10 minutes, until sides become golden. Remove from the oven and cool completely on a wire rack.

PLACE 7–8 COOKIES on a 10-inch cake plate, evenly. On the second level, place 6–7 cookies, using vanilla frosting to secure cookies together. Repeat, using less cookies and frosting as your glue for each layer, ending with one cookie. Top with more frosting and a sprinkle of mini chocolate chips for garnish if desired.

Layered Cookie
Cake

Yellow Cake with Chocolate Buttercream

2½ cups flour

3 tsp. baking powder

1 tsp. baking soda

1¼ cups sugar

pinch of Kosher salt

1 cup butter, cold and cut into cubes

3 eggs, room temperature

1 cup milk, room temperature

2 tsp. almond extract

1 tsp. vanilla bean paste (or vanilla extract)

¾ cup butter, softened

1 recipe Chocolate Buttercream (p.127)

IN A MEDIUM BOWL, combine flour, baking powder, baking soda, sugar, and salt. Stir to combine. In a separate bowl, combine eggs and milk and break each egg, stirring to combine. Add almond extract and vanilla.

USING YOUR STAND MIXER, combine butter and dry mixture and stir together on low for 1–2 minutes. Butter will be in small pea-sized pieces. Gradually add milk and egg mixture until batter comes together. Pour batter into two 9-inch cake pans lined with parchment paper and lightly greased. Bake at 350 degrees for 24–28 minutes, until toothpick comes out clean. Remove from the oven and cool completely.

PREPARE CAKE by cutting layers (optional). Frost with Chocolate Buttercream frosting on sides, middle, and top of layers.

The Crazy Larry

My friend remembers her dad, Larry, loving this cake. This is their family recipe. And the crazy thing about Larry is that he loved eating it in a bowl of milk. Thanks for sharing this great cake recipe with me!

3 cups flour

2 cups sugar

6 Tbsp. cocoa

2 tsp. baking soda

¾ cup melted shortening

2 Tbsp. vinegar

2 cups cold water

COMBINE flour, sugar, cocoa, and soda. Whisk until combined. Then add ingredients. Melt and cool shortening. Add shortening, vinegar, and water to mixture. Stir until combined. Pour into a greased 9 x 13-inch cake pan and bake at 350 degrees for 35–38 minutes. Remove from the oven and cool completely.

FROST with Minute Fudge Frosting (p.136), or any frosting you prefer.

Mexican Hot Chocolate Cake

I had a little cupcake baking contest once, and the winner made Mexican Hot Chocolate cupcakes. I knew I had to make that recipe into a cake.

3 cups flour

½ cup sugar

I cup brown sugar

I tsp. baking soda

I tsp. baking powder

¾ cup cocoa

pinch of salt

½ cup vegetable oil

1⅔ cups buttermilk

2 tsp. vanilla extract

2 tsp. cayenne pepper, or more if you like it hot

I recipe Chocolate Buttercream (p.127)

I recipe Chocolate Ganache (p.134)

IN A MEDIUM BOWL, mix together flour, sugars, baking soda, baking powder, cocoa, and salt. Stir until well combined.

IN A SEPARATE BOWL, mix together vegetable oil, buttermilk, vanilla extract, and cayenne pepper. Add wet ingredients to dry mixture and stir until combined. Do not overmix. Pour batter into three greased and parchment-lined 9-inch cake pans. Bake at 350 degrees for 23–25 minutes, until cake springs back when lightly touched. Remove from the oven and cool completely.

CUT CAKE LAYERS to make them even (p. xv). Frost middle layers only, spreading fresh berries on top of each layer of frosting. Sprinkle powdered sugar and fresh berries on top for garnish.

Chocolate Zucchini Cake

What in the world do you make with all that zucchini from your garden? Why, this chocolate cake, of course. It's moist and smooth and has a great flavor. My kids love to eat their vegetables when chocolate is involved. Don't you?

2½ cups flour

1 tsp. baking soda

1 tsp. baking powder

1 Tbsp. cinnamon

¼ cup dark cocoa

2 cups grated zucchini

¼ cup vegetable oil

¾ cup sour milk or buttermilk

2 Tbsp. vanilla paste or pure vanilla extract

pinch of salt

1 cup brown sugar

2 eggs

Chocolate Ganache (p.134)

IN A LARGE BOWL, combine, flour, baking soda and powder, cinnamon, and dark cocoa. Stir to combine and make sure cocoa is mixed evenly.

IN A SEPARATE BOWL, mix grated zucchini, oil, milk, vanilla, salt, sugar, and eggs. Gently add wet ingredients to dry mixture. Pour batter into two 9-inch greased and lined baking pans or a 9 x 13-inch pan.

BAKE AT 350 DEGREES for about 25 minutes until cake springs back when lightly touched. Remove from the oven and cool completely. Frost with Chocolate Ganache (p.134).

Wendy's Chocolate Peanut Butter Poke Cake

This recipe is not mine, but belongs to my friend, another Wendy. She loves sweets as much as I do, and she has a great name.

2½ cups flour

3 tsp. baking powder

1 tsp. baking soda

1¼ cups sugar

pinch of Kosher salt

1 cup butter, cold, cut into cubes

3 eggs, room temperature

1 cup milk, room temperature

2 tsp. almond extract

1 tsp. vanilla bean paste (or vanilla extract)

¾ cup butter, softened

1 cup creamy peanut butter

2 cups peanut butter cups, chopped

1 recipe Chocolate Buttercream (p.127)

1 (10-oz.) can sweetened condensed milk

IN A MEDIUM BOWL, combine flour, baking powder, baking soda, sugar, and salt. Stir to combine.

IN A SEPARATE BOWL, combine eggs and milk and break each egg, stirring to combine. Add almond extract and vanilla.

USING A STAND MIXER, combine butter and dry mixture and stir together on low for 1–2 minutes, until butter is in small pea-sized pieces. Gradually add milk and egg mixture until batter comes together. Pour batter into a 9 x 13-inch baking pan, lightly greased. Bake at 350 degrees for 24–28 minutes until toothpick comes out clean. Remove from the oven.

WHILE CAKE IS STILL WARM, poke holes in the top with a straw or small knife. Then pour sweetened condensed milk on cake and let soak in. While still warm, spread peanut butter on top, then Chocolate Buttercream frosting. Frosting will be soft because of warm cake. Once cake has cooled, top with peanut butter cups. Refrigerate until ready to serve.

Chocolate Sour Cream Bundt Cake

This cake is a pretty perfect combination of tang and chocolate. And more chocolate.

2 cups flour

¼ cup dark cocoa

1 tsp. baking soda

1 tsp. baking powder

pinch of salt

1 cup brown sugar

¼ cup milk

¼ cup vegetable oil

4 eggs

1 cup sour cream

1 tsp. vanilla bean paste or pure extract

½ cup semi sweet chocolate chips

Chocolate Ganache (p.134)

mini chocolate chips for garnish (optional)

IN A LARGE BOWL, combine flour, cocoa, baking soda and powder, salt, and brown sugar. Stir to combine.

IN A SEPARATE BOWL, combine milk, oil, eggs, sour cream, vanilla, and chocolate chips. Add wet ingredients to dry mixture, stirring until just combined. Do not overmix batter.

POUR BATTER into a greased and floured 10-inch Bundt pan and bake at 325 degrees for 35–40 minutes. Remove from the oven and invert pan onto baking rack. Cool for 30 minutes. Gently tap top of pan to get cake out. Top with a drizzle of Chocolate Ganache (p.134) and more chocolate chips for garnish.

Chocolate Sour Cream Bundt Cake

Chocolate Coconut Pound Cake

No matter the party or occasion you are baking this cake for, it's sure to be a winner.

2 cups flour

1 tsp. baking soda

1 tsp. baking powder

1½ cups water

8 oz. unsweetened baking chocolate, broken into pieces and divided

2 cups sugar

1 cup butter, softened

1 tsp. almond emulsion or extract

3 eggs

COMBINE flour, baking soda, and baking powder in a small bowl. Bring water to a boil. Add 6 oz. of chocolate and stir until smooth. Beat sugar, butter, and almond emulsion in a large mixer bowl until creamy. Add eggs and beat on high for 5 minutes. Beat in flour mixture, alternating with chocolate mixture. Pour into well-greased and floured Bundt pan. Bake in oven at 325 degrees for 50–60 minutes or until cake springs back when lightly touched.

COOL inverted on a wire rack completely. Drizzle with:

3 Tbsp. butter

1½ cups sifted powdered sugar

2-3 Tbsp. water

1 tsp. vanilla

MELT remaining chocolate and butter in a saucepan until melted and smooth. Remove from heat and stir in powdered sugar and water until mixture reaches desired consistency.

Black Velvet Cake

This cake is so beautiful. It's a great cake for any occasion, especially Halloween.

3 cups flour

2 cups sugar

½ cup cocoa

1 tsp. baking powder

1 tsp. baking soda

3 eggs

1½ cups milk

½ cup sour cream

2 tsp. vanilla extract

2 oz. black food coloring gel

1 recipe Vanilla Buttercream frosting (p.125) or Chocolate Buttercream (p.127)

SIFT TOGETHER flour, sugar, cocoa, baking powder, and baking soda. Set aside. In a separate bowl, mix together eggs, milk, sour cream and vanilla. Add food coloring.

MIX TOGETHER dry and wet ingredients. Do not overmix. Pour into two greased and parchment-lined round cake pans. Bake at 350 degrees for 25–27 minutes. Remove from the oven and cool completely.

FROST LAYERS, top, and sides of cooled cake. Serve.

Black Forest Mousse Cake

I like to change classics up a bit. That's just my nature—change. To this cake I added a layer of mousse for sophistication and some freshly frozen sweet cherries for garnishing. This cake is worthy of royalty.

1 ½ cup flour

⅔ cup brown sugar

⅓ cup sugar

½ cup cocoa

½ tsp. baking powder

½ tsp. baking soda

pinch of salt

2 eggs

1 ½ cup buttermilk

1 tsp. almond emulsion or extract

1 recipe Chocolate Ganache (p.134)

1 recipe Stiff Whipped Cream (p.124)

2 cups fresh or frozen cherries, plus more for garnish

IN A MEDIUM BOWL, mix together flour, sugars, cocoa, baking powder, baking soda, and salt. Stir to combine.

IN A SEPARATE BOWL, combine wet ingredients; eggs, buttermilk, and almond emulsion. Pour batter into a parchment-lined and greased 10-inch springform pan. Bake at 350 degrees for 30–35 minutes, until cake springs back when lightly touched. Let cake cool completely.

THEN FOLD half of Chocolate Ganache into Stiff Whipped Cream, creating a rich mousse. Set aside.

UNMOLD CAKE from springform pan. Spread remaining Chocolate Ganache on top and place I cup of cherries on top. Then top cake with mousse. Refrigerate until ready to serve. Top with remaining cherries.

HINT: To spread mousse tall and straight, wrap parchment paper around the sides of the cake, taping sides together to form a tall mold about an inch higher than the cake. Spread the mousse on top of cake (not sides) and place in fridge to set. Remove parchment paper from sides when ready to serve.

Black Forest Mousse Cake

Holiday Treats

Cannoli Cream Cake

I'm taking the flavor of the classic Cannoli and turning it into a delicious cake. Cake doesn't have to be plain old vanilla or chocolate anymore.

4 cups flour

2 cups sugar

1 tsp. baking soda

1 tsp. baking powder

½ cup cold butter, cut into small pieces

4 eggs

1 Tbsp. vanilla extract

1¼ cups milk

CANNOLI CREAM:

2 cups Ricotta cheese

1 cup Mascarpone cheese

1 cup powdered sugar

1 medium orange, zested

1 cup mini chocolate chips

1 recipe Stiff Whipped Cream (p.124)

MIX TOGETHER flour, sugar, baking soda, and baking powder. Cut butter pieces into flour mixture with a pastry cutter. Once butter is pea-sized, add eggs, vanilla, and milk.

POUR CAKE BATTER into two 10-inch round cake pans, greased, floured, and lined with parchment paper. Bake at 350 degrees for 25–28 minutes.

REMOVE from the oven and cool completely. Slice both cake layers in half horizontally, preparing for layering with Cannoli Cream (p. xv).

FROST middle layers with Cannoli Cream. Then frost top and sides of cake with Stiff Whipped Cream (p.124). Refrigerate until ready to serve.

Cannoli Cream Cake

White Chocolate Peppermint Swirl Cake

I wanted to do something a little more creative for a peppermint cake. After consulting with one of my sous chefs, we decided on this: a peppermint swirled Bundt cake. Lots of flavor, color, and a rich creamy white chocolate glaze.

2½ cups flour

1 cup sugar

1 tsp. baking soda

1 tsp. baking powder

pinch of salt

3 eggs

1 cup milk

½ cup sour cream

¼ cup vegetable oil

1–2 tsp. peppermint extract or peppermint oil

1 oz. red food coloring gel

GLAZE:

2 cups powdered sugar

2–4 Tbsp. heavy cream

½ tsp. peppermint extract or oil

crushed peppermint candies for garnish (optional)

IN A LARGE MIXING BOWL, combine all ingredients except red food coloring. When batter comes together, divide half into a separate bowl. Mix in red food coloring so you have a bowl of white batter and a bowl of red batter.

BUTTER AND FLOUR your 10-inch Bundt pan. Scoop both batters into the pan, alternating between red and white. Then, using a butter knife, swirl batters together. Bake at 325 degrees for 25–30 minutes, until cake is lightly brown and springs back when touched. Remove from the oven and cool for 10 minutes. Then invert onto a wire rack to cool completely.

WHISK TOGETHER powdered sugar, heavy cream, and remaining ½ tsp. peppermint extract for glaze. Drizzle on cooled Peppermint Swirl cake. Garnish with peppermint candies.

White Chocolate Peppermint Swirl Cake

Chocolate Rum Flourless Cake

One of the wonderful tasty treats I've enjoyed when on a cruise is Rum Balls. Anyone else had them before? This cake is my version of this treat, an entire cake to enjoy.

1 cup heavy cream

1 (12-oz.) pkg. dark chocolate chips

¼ cup dark cocoa

2 tsp. rum emulsion or 2 Tbsp. dark rum

1 cup brown sugar

6 eggs

½ recipe Chocolate Ganache (p.134)

HEAT HEAVY CREAM and pour over dark chocolate chips. Let stand for 2 minutes. Add dark cocoa, rum, and brown sugar. Then gently add eggs, one at a time, until cake batter is nice and smooth. Butter a 9-inch spring-form pan, and cover the bottom with aluminum foil to prevent leaking.

POUR BATTER into the pan and place in a steam bath to bake at 325 degrees for 40–42 minutes. Cool completely. Top with Chocolate Ganache.

Red, White, and Blue Pound Cake

This cake is patriotic and colorful, but fresh and light for the summer. I know., I just used the word "light" to describe a pound cake. Let's just move right along to the recipe.

½ lb. butter, softened

½ lb. vegetable shortening

2½ cups sugar

pinch of salt

½ tsp. baking soda

6 eggs

¾ cup milk

1 tsp. vanilla extract

3 cups flour

1 recipe Stiff Whipped Cream (p.124)

raspberries, strawberries and blueberries (plus 1–2 Tbsp. sugar if needed for sweetness)

CREAM TOGETHER butter, shortening, sugar, salt, and baking soda. Add eggs one at a time. Then add milk, and vanilla extract. Add flour and gently mix until just combined. Do not overmix this batter. Pour into a greased and floured 10-inch Bundt pan.

BAKE THE CAKE at 350 degrees for 60 to 90 minutes, until cake springs back when lightly touched and top is golden brown. Serve cake with a dollop of whipped cream and a spoonful of fresh berries. Maybe even some mint to be fancy.

Cranberry Upside Down Cake

A different take on the classic pineapple upside down cake, this cake is amazing and is a beautiful dark red color. I simply love this cake.

2 eggs

½ cup buttermilk

I tsp. vanilla extract

I ¾ cups sugar

I tsp. baking powder

pinch of salt

½ cup butter

½ cup orange juice

2 Tbsp. grated orange zest

I ½ cups flour

I cup fresh cranberries

I cup whole cranberry sauce

I tsp. cinnamon

½ tsp. nutmeg

IN A LARGE BOWL, mix together egg whites, buttermilk, vanilla, sugar, powder, salt, butter, orange zest, and orange juice. Batter will come together quickly. Do not overmix.

IN A SMALL BOWL, combine cranberries, cranberry sauce, cinnamon, and nutmeg.

SPREAD SAUCE into the bottom of a greased floured and parchment-lined 9 or 10-inch cake pan. Pour cake batter on top and bake at 350 degrees for 24–28 minutes, until cake is golden and springs back when touched. Remove from the oven and allow to cool completely.

Dulce de Leche Cake

I have to admit that I get my inspiration from very unusual places. While baking at a home show, an audience member asked me to do more Dulce de Leche recipes. So, since I can't seem to say no to great recipes, this recipe was created. Thank you to everyone who gives me such great ideas.

3 cups flour

1 cup brown sugar

1 cup sugar

1 tsp. baking powder

1 tsp. baking soda

pinch of salt

3 eggs

1 cup milk

½ cup sour cream or Greek yogurt

2 tsp. vanilla extract

2 (10-oz.) cans Carnation dulce de leche

1 recipe Vanilla Buttercream (p.125)

Chocolate Ganache (p.134) (optional)

SIFT TOGETHER flour, sugars, baking powder, baking soda, and salt. Set aside. In a separate bowl, mix together eggs, milk, sour cream, and vanilla. Mix together dry and wet ingredients. Do not overmix. Pour into three greased and parchment-lined 9-inch round cake pans. Bake at 350 degrees for 25–27 minutes. Remove from the oven and cool completely.

CREAM TOGETHER 1 can of dulce de leche and Vanilla Buttercream Frosting. Add up to 1 cup more powdered sugar to thicken, if necessary.

CUT THE TOP OFF THE CAKES to even out cake layers (p. xv). Spread one-third of remaining can Dulce de Leche on the first layer. Then top with frosting. Repeat and frost sides. Top cake with the final layer of Dulce de Leche. Drizzle with Chocolate Ganache (p.134) if desired for garnish.

Dulce de Leche Cake

Maple Blackberry Cake

I had the most delicious doughnut while in Montana, and I couldn't get the flavor combination out of my head. Since I could use some of this goodness in my life, I decided to make a cake out of it.

5 large egg whites

½ cup whole milk

2 tsp. vanilla extract

1¾ cup sugar

1 Tbsp. baking powder

3 cups flour

pinch of salt

1 cup butter, softened

1½ cups buttermilk

1 recipe Swiss Buttercream (p.135)

1 Tbsp. maple flavoring

2 cups blackberry preserves

fresh blackberries for garnish (optional

IN A LARGE BOWL, mix together egg whites, milk, vanilla, sugar, baking powder, flour, salt, butter, and milk. The batter will come together quickly. Do not overmix.

POUR BATTER into two greased, floured, and parchment-lined 9 or 10-inch cake pans. Bake at 350 degrees for 28–32 minutes until cake is golden and springs back when touched. Remove from the oven and cool completely.

COMBINE MAPLE FLAVORING with Swiss Buttercream Frosting. Spread half the blackberry preserves on cake layers before frosting. Frost sides, middle, and top of cake with frosting and garnish with fresh blackberries.

Root Beer Float Cake

For Ethan, who never says no to a good root beer float, or even a good root beer float cake.

4 cups flour

2 cups sugar

1 tsp. baking soda

1 tsp. baking powder

½ cup cold butter, cut into small pieces

4 eggs

1 Tbsp. root beer flavoring

1¼ cups milk

MIX TOGETHER flour, sugar, baking soda, and baking powder. Cut butter into flour mixture with a pastry cutter. Once butter is pea-sized, add eggs, root beer flavoring, and milk.

POUR CAKE BATTER into two 10-inch round cake pans, greased, floured, and lined with parchment paper. Bake at 350 degrees for 25–28 minutes. Remove from the oven and cool completely. Slice cake into halves to prepare to layer the Root Beer Cream.

ROOT BEER CREAM:

1 pkg. whipped topping mix

½ cup root beer

MIX WHIPPED TOPPING MIX and root beer until rich and creamy. Frost cake and serve.

Whole Wheat Cinnamon Roll Cake

The challenge here was to make a sweet treat into something a little bit more healthy. This is a cake I actually make for breakfast now and then. I know the amount of steps can seem overwhelming, but you can actually make this cake in under 10 minutes, then put it in the oven. Simple.

2½ cups whole wheat flour

3 eggs (or ½ cup applesauce)

¾ cup grapeseed or vegetable oil (I love grapeseed—It has a really nice nutty flavor)

⅔ cup sugar

1 tsp. cinnamon

1 tsp. baking soda

1 tsp. baking powder

¾ cup milk

pinch of salt

TOPPING:

1 cup brown sugar

½ cup butter, softened

1 tsp. cinnamon

2 Tbsp. grapeseed oil or vegetable oil

GLAZE:

2 cups powdered sugar

2 Tbsp. milk

MIX TOGETHER flour, eggs, oil, sugar, cinnamon, baking soda, baking powder, milk, and salt. Pour into a greased 9 × 13-inch pan. Set aside. Next, make the topping by combining brown sugar, butter, cinnamon, and oil.

STIR TOGETHER to make a paste, then drop on top of cake batter by spoonfuls. Swirl topping into the cake batter using a knife. Bake at 350 degrees for 24–26 minutes until cake is done. Remove from the oven and cool for 5 minutes while you make the glaze. Then drizzle glaze over warm cake and serve. Yum.

VARIATION: Pumpkin Cinnamon Roll

Add 1 cup pureed pumpkin to the batter.

Napoleon

This cake is for Danielle. I'm so glad you had a good feeling about this cake. This classic French dessert is something really special for you to serve at any occasion. I have a good feeling about this cake too.

2 boxes puff pastry (4 sheets total)

1 pint heavy whipping cream

3 Tbsp. Bird's Custard Powder

2½ cups powdered sugar, divided

1 tsp. vanilla extract

4 oz. semi-sweet chocolate

2–3 Tbsp. boiling water

½ cup fruit preserves (optional)

9-in. springform pan

LET PUFF PASTRY DEFROST 20 minutes before unrolling and cutting. Place pastry sheet on a parchment-lined baking sheet. Trace a 9-inch round circle using your springform pan. Cut with a sharp knife, then pierce with a fork multiple times to let air escape while baking. Remove scraps from baking sheet. Repeat until 4 rounds have been cut and pierced. Then bake rounds on your parchment-lined baking sheet for 20 minutes until crispy and fluffy. Remove from the oven and cool completely.

SLIGHTLY FLATTEN PASTRY with a rolling pin to uniform thickness. While pastry cools, assemble custard cream. Whip heavy cream until stiff peaks form. Add ½ cup powdered sugar and Bird's Custard Powder. Fold into cream. Add vanilla extract and fold until combined. Set aside.

TO ASSEMBLE: place a round pastry in the bottom of the springform pan. Spread 2–3 Tbsp. fruit preserves, then one-third of the custard cream. Repeat until you end up with a pastry on top.

WHISK TOGETHER glaze: remaining powdered sugar, boiling water, and vanilla. Spread on top of final pastry.

MELT CHOCOLATE for garnishing. Cool slightly. Drizzle chocolate or pipe on glaze in straight, parallel lines, about 1 inch apart. Then, with a butter knife, pull a line horizontally across the parallel chocolate lines to create a design. Refrigerate overnight for best results, or at least 2 hours.

HINT: Apricot, raspberry, lemon, and orange preserves are all amazing with this dessert.

Napoleon

Peanut Butter Sheet Cake

There's no such thing as too much butter, cheese, or peanut butter. This cake is full of peanut butter flavor. And of course, peanut butter marshmallow frosting tops it all off.

2 cups flour

1½ cups brown sugar

½ tsp. baking soda

pinch of salt

1 cup water

¾ cup butter

¾ cup creamy peanut butter

2 eggs

½ cup buttermilk

1 tsp. vanilla extract

MARSHMALLOW FROSTING:

⅔ cup sugar

⅓ cup milk

2 Tbsp. butter

½ cup peanut butter

½ cup mini marshmallows

MIX TOGETHER flour, sugar, baking soda, salt, water, butter, peanut butter, eggs, buttermilk, and vanilla. Combine until batter is smooth, about 2 minutes. Do not overmix. Pour into a greased 15 x 10 x 1-inch jelly roll pan. Bake at 350 degrees for 18–24 minutes, until cake springs back when lightly touched. Remove from the oven and cool for 10 minutes before pouring frosting on top.

WHILE THE CAKE is cooking, made the frosting. Bring to a boil: sugar, milk, butter, and peanut butter. Remove from the heat and add mini marshmallows and vanilla and stir until melted and smooth. Pour over warm cake.

Red Velvet Cake

Red Velvet Cake

A wonderful southern tradition. I love cakes that are tasty, but cakes that are beautiful and tasty are my favorite. This cake is so beautiful. But I'm a little partial to this cake because of its color. I love red. I'm really excited about this recipe. Can you tell?

3 cups flour

2 cups sugar

½ cup cocoa

1 tsp. baking powder

1 tsp. baking soda

3 eggs

1½ cups milk

½ cup sour cream or Greek yogurt

2 tsp. vanilla extract

4 Tbsp. red velvet emulsion or 4 oz. red food coloring gel or liquid

1 recipe Cream Cheese Buttercream (p.138)

SIFT TOGETHER flour, sugar, cocoa, baking powder, and baking soda. Set aside. In a separate bowl, mix together eggs, milk, sour cream, and vanilla. Add red velvet emulsion.

MIX TOGETHER dry and wet ingredients. Do not overmix. Pour into three greased and parchment-lined 9-inch round cake pans. Bake at 350 degrees for 25–27 minutes. Remove from the oven and cool completely. Frost layers, top, and sides of cooled cake with Cream Cheese Buttercream (p.138).

Vintage Basket Cake

This was the first cake I made for this book. I had seen it in a copy of an old cook book and wanted to give it a fresh, new look—for it's certainly a cake to entertain with.

1¼ cups sugar, divided

½ cup butter

4 egg whites

1 tsp. vanilla extract

1 tsp. almond emulsion or extract

1½ cups flour

2 tsp. baking powder

⅓ cup milk

4 egg whites

2 cups fresh berries for garnish (blackberries, strawberries, raspberries, blueberries)

1 recipe Stiffed Whipped Cream (p. 124)

CREAM TOGETHER ¾ cup sugar and butter until light and fluffy, about 2 minutes. Then add the egg whites, vanilla, and almond flavoring, and combine. Then add flour, baking powder, and milk. Batter will be a little thicker.

POUR THE BATTER into a round 9-inch greased and parchment-lined cake pan or springform pan. Bake the cake at 350 degrees for 28–32 minutes. Remove the cake from the oven and cool slightly.

MEANWHILE, whisk together egg whites for 3–4 minutes, until stiff peaks form. Then gradually add remaining sugar and mix another minute or so. Top warm cake with meringue, making the sides higher than the middle to make a basket for the berries. Bake at 400 degrees for 4–5 minutes until meringue is golden brown. Remove from the oven and cool completely. Sprinkle 2 tablespoons sugar on top of fresh berries to sweeten slightly. Spread a layer of sweet whipped cream on top of cooled meringue, then fill "basket" of cake with an assortment of fresh berries.

Brown Derby Cake

According to my research, this cake's origin is close to New York City—The Jersey Shore, to be exact. It's a nice chocolate cake with a cream filling and fresh strawberries, bananas, and peaches. Fresh, rich, and super delicious.

3 cups flour

½ cup sugar

1 cup brown sugar

1 tsp. baking soda

1 tsp. baking powder

¾ cup cocoa

pinch of salt

½ cup vegetable oil

1⅔ cups buttermilk

2 tsp. vanilla extract

1 recipe Stiff Whipped Cream (p.124)

2 cups fresh strawberries, sliced

2 cups fresh peaches, peeled and sliced

2 bananas, peeled and sliced

whole strawberries for garnish (optional)

IN A MEDIUM BOWL, mix together flour, sugars, baking soda, baking powder, cocoa, and salt. Stir until well combined.

IN A SEPARATE BOWL, mix together vegetable oil, buttermilk, and vanilla. Add wet ingredients to dry ingredients and stir until combined. Do not overmix. Pour Batter equally into three greased and parchment-lined

9-inch cake pans. Bake at 350 degrees for 23–25 minutes, until cake springs back when lightly touched. Remove from the oven and cool completely.

CUT EACH COOLED LAYER in half horizontally. Layer cooled cake with Stiff Whipped Cream (p.124) and spread evenly with half of the fresh strawberries, peaches, and bananas. Repeat with final layer, then frost the entire cake with remaining Stiff Whipped Cream. Top with chocolate shavings and whole strawberries if desired.

Sweet Potato Cake

My son has requested this cake so many times, I've lost track. It's a fantastic cake with a uniquely soft texture, much like a thick pie.

2 lb. sweet potatoes, cooked, peeled, and pureed

1 ¼ cups unsweetened applesauce

¼ cup dark brown sugar

4 eggs

½ tsp. fresh ginger

2 tsp. vanilla extract

2 cups flour

2 tsp. baking powder

1 tsp. salt

1 Tbsp. cinnamon

1 tsp. nutmeg

COMBINE sweet potatoes, applesauce, sugar, eggs, ginger, and vanilla until combined. In a separate bowl, mix together baking powder, salt, cinnamon, and nutmeg. Combine wet and dry ingredients, stirring until all ingredients are mixed well. Pour into two 9-inch greased cake pans. Bake at 350 degrees for 25 minutes, until cake springs back when lightly touched. Cool completely.

FROST with Brown Sugar Cinnamon Buttercream Frosting (see recipe on following page). Garnish with candied pecans if desired. Refrigerate leftovers, covered, for up to a week.

Brown Sugar Cinnamon Buttercream Frosting

½ cup dark brown sugar

1 tsp. cinnamon

2 lb. powdered sugar

1 cup unsalted butter, softened

3–4 Tbsp. heavy cream

CREAM TOGETHER butter and sugars until completely combined and fluffy. Frost your cooled cake and serve.

Waldorf Cake

Get ready for a complicated story behind this cake: My friend Ann's mom's cousin's wife made this cake when she stayed with them while her Grandma was sick—and it's become a family tradition. It's a very moist cake with lots of flavor. And really, when it comes down to it, it doesn't matter if you understand where it came from. Just give it a try and it may just become a family tradition for you too.

2¼ cups cake flour

1 tsp. salt

½ cup shortening

1½ cups sugar

2 eggs

2 oz. red food coloring

2 Tbsp. cocoa

1 cup buttermilk

1 tsp. vanilla extract

1 Tbsp. white vinegar

1 tsp. baking soda

SIFT AND MEASURE flour and add salt. Cream shortening, sugar, and eggs. Mix coloring and cocoa into a paste and add to creamed mixture. Add buttermilk, then add flour mixture and vanilla to creamed mixture. Quickly mix vinegar and soda together and add to batter. Do no overmix after adding soda mixture.

BAKE AT 350 for 30 minutes in two 9-inch round pans, greased and lined with parchment paper.

Icing

3 Tbsp. cake flour

1 cup milk

1 cup sugar

½ tsp. salt

1 cup butter

1 Tbsp. vanilla

MIX AND COOK flour and milk until thick over medium heat. Cream sugar, salt, and butter. Add vanilla. Add flour mixture and beat until smooth. Frost layers and top of cake.

Pig Pickling Cake

Oh. My. Goodness. There are so many great recipes that are considered "vintage," but there is no reason why they can't be made all the time. This cake was a favorite with my wonderful taste testers.

4 cups flour

2 cups sugar

1 tsp. baking soda

1 tsp. baking powder

½ cup cold butter, cut into small pieces

4 eggs

1 Tbsp. vanilla extract

1¼ cups milk

1 (11-oz.) can of mandarin oranges with juice

MIX TOGETHER flour, sugar, baking soda, and baking powder. Cut butter into flour mixture with a pastry cutter. Once butter is pea-sized, add eggs, vanilla, milk, and mandarin oranges.

POUR CAKE BATTER into two 10-inch round cake pans, greased, floured, and lined with parchment paper. Bake at 350 degrees for 25–28 minutes. Remove from the oven and allow to cool completely.

Frosting

1 (4-oz.) pkg. instant vanilla pudding mix

1 (12-oz.) can crushed pineapple, drained and dry

1 (9-oz.) tub cool whip

½ cup finely chopped walnuts

ADD instant vanilla pudding mix to pineapple and fold in cool whip. Add walnuts. Frost and layer cake and place in fridge to pickle for 3 days—if it lasts that long!

Snickerdoodle Cake

Snickerdoodle Cake

Snickerdoodle cookies are one of my kids' favorite treats, so I thought I'd make this cake just for them. It's so much fun and is a great surprise cake for any party—or just because.

5 large egg whites

½ cup whole milk

2 tsp. vanilla extract

2¼ cups sugar, divided

1 Tbsp. baking powder

3 cups flour

pinch of salt

1 cup butter, softened

1½ cups buttermilk

2 Tbsp. cinnamon

1 recipe Swiss Buttercream (p.135)

IN A LARGE BOWL, mix together egg whites, milk, vanilla, 1¾ cups sugar, baking powder, flour, salt, butter, and milk. The batter will come together quickly. Do not overmix.

POUR BATTER into two greased, floured, and parchment-lined 9 or 10-inch cake pans. Bake at 350 degrees for 28–32 minutes, until cake is golden and springs back when touched.

REMOVE FROM THE OVEN and cool completely. In a small bowl, combine remaining ½ cup sugar and cinnamon. Set aside. Combine 1 tablespoon cinnamon with Swiss Buttercream Frosting. Frost sides, middle, and top of cake with frosting and sprinkle the top and sides with the cinnamon sugar for garnish.

Amazin' Raisin Cake

This is a recipe from a good friend, Carol—a recipe her family has made for generations. Thanks, Carol, for sharing this great recipe with me. And don't let the mayonnaise fool you. It's an older trick that makes the cake taste amazing. Don't substitute it for anything else.

3 cups flour

2 cups sugar

1 cup mayonnaise

⅓ cup milk

2 eggs

2 tsp. baking soda

1 ½ tsp. cinnamon

½ tsp. nutmeg

½ tsp. salt

¼ tsp. ground cloves

3 cups chopped, peeled apples

1 cup raisins

½ cup walnuts, coarsely chopped

GREASE AND FLOUR one 9 x 13-inch pan. In a large bowl, beat the first 10 ingredients for 2 minutes. Stir in apples, raisins, and walnuts. Pour into a pan and bake at 350 degrees for 45 minutes, or until done.

TOP with Stiff Whipped Cream (p.124) or Cream Cheese Buttercream (p.138).

Coconut Cream Cake

WARNING: This cake is addictive. I am not responsible for the amount of cake you consume. It's amazing. It's melt-in-your-mouth creamy.

5 large egg whites

½ cup whole milk

I Tbsp. coconut extract

1¾ cups sugar

I Tbsp. baking powder

3 cups flour

pinch of salt

I cup butter, softened

I (13-oz.) can coconut milk (1½ cups)

2 tsp. coconut extract

I recipe Swiss Buttercream (p.135)

I cup sweetened shredded coconut, toasted

IN A LARGE BOWL, mix together egg whites, milk, coconut extract, sugar, baking powder, salt, butter, and coconut milk. Batter will come together quickly. Do not overmix. Pour batter into a greased, floured, and 2 parchment-lined 9 or 10-inch cake pan. Bake at 350 degrees for 28–32 minutes, until cake is golden and springs back when touched.

REMOVE FROM THE OVEN and cool completely. Cream together remaining coconut extract and Swiss Buttercream frosting. Frost sides, middle, and top of cake with frosting and sprinkle the top with toasted coconut for garnish.

HINT: For coconut lovers, you can increase the coconut flavor in the frosting and cake with up to I more teaspoon of extract, if desired.

Animal Print Cakes

Giraffe Animal Print Swiss Roll

It must be in my nature, but I love animal print. Why not make a cake out of it? It's more simple than you would think—just a few extra steps will make your cake extraordinary. And trust me, it's going to be a conversation piece at your next party.

⅔ cup sugar

4 eggs, separated

⅔ cup plus ½ cup flour, divided

pinch of salt

1 tsp. baking powder

2 Tbsp. water

1 tsp. vanilla

½ cup cocoa

1 quart ice cream, softened, or 1 recipe Stiff Whipped Cream (p.124)

½ recipe Chocolate Ganache (p.134)

PREHEAT the oven to 375 degrees. Cream together ⅓ cup sugar and egg yolks until light and fluffy, about 2–3 minutes. Add ⅔ cup flour, salt, baking powder, water, and vanilla. Stir to combine. Do not overmix. Batter will be thick.

IN A SEPARATE BOWL, whisk together egg whites until light and fluffy. Gradually add remaining sugar until stiff peaks form.

COMBINE both batter and egg whites, starting with ⅓ of the egg whites. Gently fold them into the batter, then continue until all remaining egg whites are combined. Remove ⅔ cup batter and place in a separate small bowl. Add remaining ½ cup flour. Mixture will be thick as you stir it together. Pour this batter into a small plastic bag. Set aside.

MIX COCOA into the batter bowl, gently folding to combine completely. Set aside. Line a 15 x 10 x 1-inch jelly roll pan with parchment paper, greasing thoroughly. Take your small plastic bag of thick batter and cut a small piece off the end—less is more in this case. Squeeze batter onto the greased parchment paper in Giraffe print lines. Fill the entire pan with squares of print. Place in the oven for 3 minutes to allow lines to set.

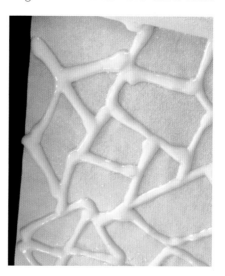

REMOVE FROM THE OVEN and pour chocolate cake batter over the top, spreading carefully over Giraffe print. Put cake back in the oven to bake for a remaining 11-12 minutes. Remove from the oven and cool for 10 minutes.

ON A KITCHEN TOWEL just larger than the pan, dust powdered sugar lightly. Peel the parchment paper off the warm cake and place, decorative side down, on the towel. Roll tightly using the towel as your guide. (The powdered sugar will keep the cake from sticking to the towel.) This will set cake for easier rolling later. Let cool, rolled up, for another 20 minutes at least.

UNROLL COOLED CAKE. It will remain a little curved still—that's ideal. Then spread filling (ice cream or Stiff Whipped Cream) on top, all the way to the edges.

THEN ROLL CAKE back up tightly again. Some filling will come out the end—that's okay. Wrap rolled cake with parchment paper and aluminum foil to seal tightly. Place in the freezer for 30 minutes to harden. Remove from the freezer

20 minutes before serving. Cut into 1 to 2-inch pieces for serving. This cake can be made up to one week in advance.

Variation: Zebra Animal Print Swiss Roll

I can't just have one animal print cake. I had to make two.

⅔ cup sugar, divided

4 eggs, separated

⅔ cup plus ¼ cup flour

pinch of salt

1 tsp. baking powder

2 Tbsp. water

1 tsp. vanilla

¼ cup cocoa

1 quart ice cream, softened, or 1 recipe Stiff Whipped Cream (p.124)

½ recipe Chocolate Ganache (p.134)

PREHEAT YOUR OVEN to 375 degrees. Cream together ⅓ cup sugar and egg yolks until light and fluffy for 2–3 minutes. Add ⅔ cup flour, salt, baking powder, water, and vanilla. Stir to combine. Do not overmix. Batter will be thick.

IN A SEPARATE BOWL, whisk together egg whites until light and fluffy. Gradually add remaining sugar until stiff peaks form.

COMBINE batter and egg whites, starting with ⅓ of the egg whites. Gently fold into batter, then continue until remaining egg whites are combined. Remove ⅔ cup batter and place in a separate small bowl. Add ¼ cup flour and ¼ cup cocoa. Mixture will be thick as you stir it together. Place this thick batter into a small plastic bag. Set aside.

PREPARE YOUR PAN: Line a 15 x 10 x 1-inch jelly roll pan with parchment paper, greasing thoroughly. Cut a small piece off one end of the bag—in this case, less is more. Squeeze batter onto the greased parchment paper in Zebra print lines, horizontally along the longest part of the pan. Fill entire pan with lines of print, touching some together. Place in the oven for 3 minutes to allow lines to set.

REMOVE from the oven and pour vanilla cake batter over the top, spreading carefully over the Zebra print. Put back in the oven to bake for a remaining 11–12 minutes. Remove cake from the oven and cool for 10 minutes.

ON A KITCHEN TOWEL just larger than the pan, dust powdered sugar lightly. Peel parchment paper off warm cake and place, decorative side down, on the towel. Roll tightly, using the towel as your guide. This will set cake for easier rolling later. Let cool, rolled up, for another 20 minutes at least.

UNROLL COOLED CAKE. It will remain a little curved still—that's ideal. Then spread filling (ice cream or Stiff Whipped Cream on top, all the way to the edges.

THEN ROLL CAKE back up tightly again. Some filling will come out the end—that's okay. Wrap rolled cake with parchment paper and aluminum foil to seal tightly. Place in the freezer for 30 minutes to harden. Remove from the freezer 20 minutes before serving. Cut into 1 to 2-inch pieces for serving. This cake can be made up to one week in advance.

Icing *on the* Big Cakes

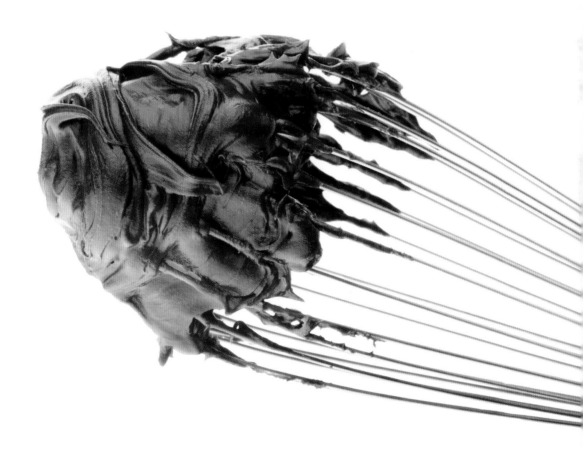

Stiff Whipped Cream

This creamy frosting offers a lot of flexibility to decorating and filling your cake. It's perfect for making so many beautiful cakes.

1 pint heavy whipping cream

½ cup powdered sugar

1 Tbsp. cornstarch

WHIP HEAVY CREAM until stiff peaks form, on high for 2–3 minutes. Fold in sugar and cornstarch until combined. Frost cake.

MAKES ABOUT 3 CUPS

Vanilla Buttercream

The classic frosting choice for any grande finale on your cake.

½ cup butter, room temperature

3¾ cups powdered sugar, sifted

3–4 Tbsp. milk or cream

2 tsp. vanilla extract

PLACE BUTTER in a large mixing bowl. Beat until light and fluffy, about 30 seconds. Stop the mixer before adding sugar or you will have a large mess to clean up.

ADD SUGAR, 3 tablespoons milk or cream, and vanilla extract. Beat frosting on low, increasing your speed until frosting is nice and creamy. Add up to 1 or more tablespoons milk if frosting is too thick.

MAKES ABOUT 3 CUPS

Chocolate
Buttercream

Chocolate Buttercream

Chocolate + Cream + Butter = Priceless

½ cup butter, room temperature

3¾ cups powdered sugar, sifted

3–4 Tbsp. milk or cream

2 tsp. vanilla extract

⅓ cup cocoa

PLACE BUTTER in a large mixing bowl. Beat until light and fluffy, about 30 seconds. Stop the mixer before adding cocoa and sugar or you will have a large mess to clean up. Add sugar, cocoa, 3 tablespoons milk or cream, and vanilla extract.

BEAT FROSTING, starting on low, and add up to 1 or more tablespoons milk if frosting is too thick.

MAKES ABOUT 3 CUPS

Fruit Buttercream

A fruity buttercream frosting to top or fill any of your cakes.

½ cup butter, room temperature

3¾ cups powdered sugar, sifted

½ cup crushed freeze-dried fruit (peaches, raspberries, strawberries, blueberries)

3–4 Tbsp. milk or cream

2 tsp. vanilla extract

PLACE BUTTER in a large mixing bowl. Beat until light and fluffy, about 30 seconds.

STOP THE MIXER before adding sugar or you will have a large mess to clean up. Add sugar, 3 tablespoons milk, and vanilla extract. Beat frosting, starting on slow and increasing your speed until frosting is nice and creamy. Add up to 1 or more tablespoons of milk if frosting is too thick.

MAKES ABOUT 3 CUPS

Maple Glaze

I could think of a million and one things to drizzle this glaze onto.

2½ cups powdered sugar

2-3 Tbsp. heavy cream

2 tsp. maple flavoring

WHISK TOGETHER all ingredients until no lumps are visible, for 2–3 minutes. Cover with plastic wrap to keep from hardening until ready to use.

MAKES ABOUT 3 CUPS

Lemon Buttercream

Fresh and bright, this frosting really shines with lemony goodness on your cake.

½ cup butter, room temperature

3¾ cups powdered sugar, sifted

3 medium lemons, zested

3–4 Tbsp. milk or cream

1 tsp. lemon oil or lemon extract

PLACE BUTTER in a large mixing bowl. Beat until light and fluffy, about 30 seconds. Stop the mixer before adding sugar or you will have a large mess to clean up.

ADD SUGAR, 3 tablespoons milk, and lemon extract. Beat frosting, starting on slow and increasing your speed until frosting is nice and creamy. Add lemon zest and up to 1 or more tablespoons milk if frosting is too thick.

MAKES ABOUT 3 CUPS

Almond Glaze

I love this glaze. It's the perfect combination of almond and cream, especially when you use an emulsion.

2½ cups powdered sugar

2–3 Tbsp. heavy cream

2 tsp. almond emulsion or extract

WHISK TOGETHER all ingredients until no lumps are visible, for 2–3 minutes. Cover with plastic wrap to keep from hardening until ready to use.

MAKES ABOUT 3 CUPS

Peanut Butter Buttercream

You can never have too much peanut butter in your frosting.

1 cup peanut butter (chunky or smooth—I prefer smooth)

½ cup butter, room temperature

2 cups powdered sugar

3–4 Tbsp. milk or cream

1 tsp. vanilla extract

COMBINE BUTTER AND PEANUT BUTTER in a large bowl mixing together until light and fluffy. Stop the mixer before adding sugar. Add sugar, 3 tablespoons milk, and vanilla. Start slow and mix together, gradually increasing the speed. Mix until smooth and creamy. Add 1 or more tablespoons milk if the frosting is too thick.

MAKES ABOUT 3 CUPS

Raspberry Glaze

This glaze is one of my favorites. But don't tell the others!

2½ cups powdered sugar

2–3 Tbsp. heavy cream

2 tsp. raspberry extract

¼ cup crushed freeze-dried raspberries

WHISK TOGETHER all ingredients until no lumps are visible, about 2–3 minutes. Cover with plastic wrap to keep from hardening until ready to use.

MAKES ABOUT 3 CUPS

Chocolate Ganache

You will make this so much, you'll know the recipe by heart. It's one of those great "use it on everything" frostings.

1 cup heavy whipping cream

12 oz. semi-sweet chocolate chunks or chips

HEAT CREAM in a saucepan until it comes to a boil. Remove cream and pour over chocolate in a mixing bowl. Stir to mix together. You can pour it over cakes warm, or allow to cool slightly and spread like frosting.

MAKES ABOUT 3 CUPS

Swiss Buttercream

I promise you won't be disappointed if you take an few minutes to prepare this frosting. It's out-of-this-world good. If you're looking for a really decadent buttercream frosting, this is it.

8 egg whites, room temperature

1½ cups sugar

1½ lb. unsalted butter, softened but cool

¾ cup vegetable shortening, softened

2 tsp. vanilla

2 lb. powdered sugar

HEAT SUGAR and egg whites in a double boiler until sugar dissolves. Remove from the heat and beat on high in a mixer until stiff peaks form. Beat in butter, about 3 tablespoons at a time. Then add powdered sugar. The frosting may look like it's curdled, or coming apart but it will come together within a few minutes. Once frosting is done, add vanilla or other flavoring and mix for 1–2 more minutes.

IF YOU WANT TO ADD COLOR, be sure to use gel food coloring. Store at room temperature for up to 2 days, or in the refrigerator for up to 1 week.

VARIATIONS:

CHOCOLATE: Add 8 ounces of melted, cooled dark chocolate after mixing frosting. Mix until combined.

PEANUT BUTTER: Add up to 2 cups creamy peanut butter after mixing frosting. Mix until combined.

CARAMEL: Add 10 ounces Dulce de Leche after mixing frosting. Mix until combined.

MAKES ABOUT 4 CUPS

Minute Fudge Frosting

This frosting really tastes like fudge and it will be a rich topping to your cakes.

2 cups sugar

⅓ cup light corn syrup

½ cup shortening

½ cup milk

2 oz. baking chocolate or 6 oz. semi sweet chocolate chips

¼ tsp. salt

1 tsp. vanilla

ADD ALL INGREDIENTS except vanilla in a saucepan. Stir over low heat until boiling. Boil 1 minute.

REMOVE FROM HEAT and cool. Add vanilla. Beat until it reaches consistency to spread by hand.

MAKES ABOUT 3 CUPS

Almond Buttercream

½ cup butter, room temperature

3¾ cups powdered sugar, sifted

3–4 Tbsp. milk or cream

2 tsp. almond emulsion or extract

PLACE BUTTER in a large mixing bowl. Beat until light and fluffy, about 30 seconds.

STOP THE MIXER before adding sugar or you will have a large mess to clean up. Add sugar, 3 tablespoons milk, and vanilla extract. Beat frosting, starting on slow and increasing speed until frosting is nice and creamy. Add up to 1 or more tablespoons milk if frosting is too thick.

MAKES ABOUT 3 CUPS

Cream Cheese Buttercream

A classic frosting. Another of my favorites.

8 oz. cream cheese, softened

½ cup butter, softened

3¾ cups powdered sugar

1 tsp. vanilla

BEAT CREAM CHEESE and butter until smooth and light. Stop the mixer and add sugar and vanilla extract. Start mixer on slow and gradually increase speed until frosting is fluffy. Frost and refrigerate.

MAKES ABOUT 3 CUPS

Coconut Buttercream

You can't really ever have enough coconut.

½ cup butter, room temperature

3¾ cups powdered sugar, sifted

3–4 Tbsp. coconut milk or cream

2 tsp. coconut extract

PLACE BUTTER in a large mixing bowl. Beat until light and fluffy for about 30 seconds. Stop the mixer before adding sugar or you will have a large mess to clean up. Add sugar, 3 tablespoons coconut milk, and coconut extract.

BEAT FROSTING starting on slow and gradually increase speed until frosting is nice and creamy. Add up to 1 or more tablespoons of coconut milk if frosting is too thick.

MAKES ABOUT 3 CUPS

Recipe Index

recipe index

recipe index

About the Author

WENDY L. PAUL has been cooking and baking for many years. She enjoys writing recipes and creating easy-to-make desserts and dinners. Occasionally, when she's not baking, she enjoys a little retail therapy at her favorite consignment stores. Her baking skills have been featured on numerous morning TV shows and news programs. When Wendy is working on a project—whether home improvement, a new recipe, or shopping at a craft store—she is truly happy. She is the bestselling author of *101 Gourmet Cupcakes in 10 Minutes*, *101 Gourmet Cookies for Everyone*, *101 Gourmet Cake Bites*, and *101 Gourmet Ice Cream Creations for Every Craving*. She and her husband, Brian, live in Utah with their four children. For more information, visit her website:

www.wendypaulcreations.com

Also by Wendy Paul

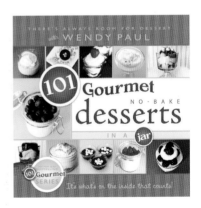

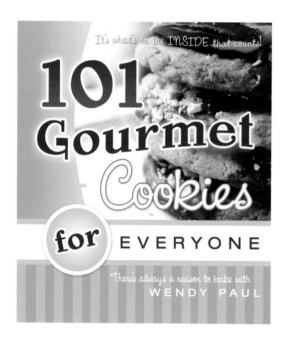

BESTSELLING AUTHOR Wendy Paul is back with a recipe collection of gourmet cookies. Whether you're watching your waistline, eating vegan, looking for a gluten-free treat, or ignoring calories, you'll find something for you in *101 Gourmet Cookies for Everyone* that not only looks great but tastes great too! These fast, easy, and foolproof recipes are sure to satisfy all your cookie cravings. You'll love the

Rosemary and Lavender Shortbread

Orange Chocolate Crinkles

Almond Cranberry

Peanut Butter Bliss

And more!

YOU'LL ALSO FIND recipes for delectable brownies and bars. With step-by-step instructions and numerous tips for success, baking has never been faster or easier. So go ahead, find your favorite recipe, and start baking. Your family and friends will thank you for these wonderful home-baked masterpieces.

EVERYONE LOVES A CUPCAKE! But not many people have the time or know-how to create gourmet masterpieces. Now even the most novice baker can make delicious cupcakes with the ease and convenience of using a cake mix! With step-by-step recipes and numerous tips for success, baking gourmet cupcakes has never been faster or easier.

EACH MOUTH-WATERING full-color photograph showcases the artfully decorated treats, such as

Strawberry Cheesecake

Key Lime Pie

Chocolate Caramel Surprise

Whether it's for a birthday party, a holiday, or just because, there's a cupcake recipe for every occasion.

YOU'VE SEEN THEM in bakeries, you've tasted their sugary sweetness, and now you can make your very own gourmet cake bites, cake balls, and cake pops right in your kitchen! Ever wondered what goes into those little dollops of goodness? Find out in the newest title from bestselling author and dessert diva, Wendy Paul. Fall in love at first BITE with these tempting treats.

Key Lime Pie

Even More S'more

Dark Chocolate Truffle

French Toast

And More!

Looking good and tasting even better, cake bites are the perfect way to celebrate anniversaries, birthdays, and holidays or make any day a special occasion! With gorgeous photographs, easy-to-follow instructions, and lots of helpful hints, these recipes are perfect for novice bakers and seasoned chefs alike—even kids can get in on the fun! But be careful—treats this tasty and good-looking are sure to disappear fast!

BESTSELLING AUTHOR and not-so-evil dessert genius Wendy Paul knows exactly what goes best with cupcakes, cookies, and cake bite—it's ice cream! And with her foolproof process and handy tips and tricks, you'll soon be creating your very own homemade ice cream, toppings, and treats!

ENJOY ALL THE DELICIOUS FLAVORS, INCLUDING

Pink Lemonade

Triple Berry

Mango Lime

Mint Truffle

Burnt Almond Fudge

PLUS THERE'S A WHOLE collection of holiday treats and specialty sweets like fried ice cream for those extra-special occasions. Imagine creating the ice cream of your dreams with all the toppings, syrups, and more! With *101 Gourmet Ice Cream Creations* you'll soon have the whole family wanting to scream for ice cream!

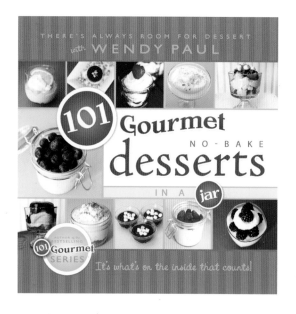

DESSERTS CAN BE QUICK AND EASY! Wendy Paul's dessert jar creations are the freshest and simplest way to present delicious flavors—and add the perfect creative touch to any gathering.

TRY THESE SWEET RECIPES

Lemonade Pie

Mint Brownie Trifle

Crème Brûlée

Triple Berry Russian Cream

WENDY PAUL has already won over our taste buds with *101 Gourmet Cupcakes in 10 Minutes*, *101 Gourmet Cake Bites*, and *101 Gourmet Cookies for Everyone*, and now she's at it again with *101 Gourmet No-Bake Desserts in a Jar*. With easy-to-follow instructions and delightful photographs, these recipes won't allow your sweet tooth to rest. So bottoms up! Make dessert the true delight of the party.

0 26575 13880 1